It Takes a
CHURCH
to Raise a
VILLAGE

It Takes a
CHURCH
to Raise a
VILLAGE

DR. MARVA MITCHELL

Treasure House

An Imprint of

Destiny Image® Publishers, Inc.
P.O. Box 310
Shippensburg, PA 17257-0310

"For where your treasure is, there will your heart be also."
Matthew 6:21

ISBN 0-7684-3035-6

For Worldwide Distribution
Printed in the U.S.A.

First Printing: 2001   Second Printing: 2001

This book and all other Destiny Image, Revival Press, MercyPlace, Fresh Bread, Destiny Image Fiction, and Treasure House books are available at Christian bookstores and distributors worldwide.

For a U.S. bookstore nearest you, call **1-800-722-6774**.
For more information on foreign distributors, call **717-532-3040**.
Or reach us on the Internet: **www.destinyimage.com**

Dedication

To the memory of my departed husband, who went home to be with the Lord on April 16, 1998. He fought a good fight and he finished his course. He was a father in the village and an example to the Body of Christ. For 32 years we worked side by side to raise our village and to impact the lives of families, beginning in our own home. He was the greatest man I have ever known, second to Jesus Christ.

To my seven children who stand by my side and give their total support to the visions that God has placed in my life. To Willie, Marvin, Sharon, Paul, Monica, Joe, and Miracle—the magnificent seven.

To Bishop John Davis—you are a great inspiration to me and your village.

To Revival Center Ministries International—you are truly my family and a blessing in my life. I love you for your faithfulness and support.

Endorsements

Any church leader or layperson who seriously prays for the restoration of his or her community should read Dr. Mitchell's book with great diligence. The concept is a cutting-edge description of how we can better pierce our community and effect a massive and comprehensive change. I think it should be recommended reading, from Sunday schools to seminaries.

Bishop T.D. Jakes, Sr.
Founder, The Potter's House of Dallas, Inc.

This insightful and provocative treatise captures the heart, the passion, and the vision of one of America's foremost experts in community transformation and empowerment. It is a must-read for any serious advocate of holistic and self-sustaining communities.

Bishop Harold Calvin Ray
Founder and CEO
The National Center for Faith Based Initiatives

God has certainly spoken to the heart of our dear friend, Marva Mitchell. It is our job as leaders to work, pray, and get behind this concept of hope. What a revealing assessment of the condition of our nation! This book should be the awareness wake-up call to the world—we hope it will be printed in many languages.

Pastors Lawrence and Darlene Bishop
Solid Rock Church
Monroe, OH

Through her love for Christ, Dr. Mitchell has called the Church to change people's lives by changing the community in which they live. Her proven leadership and success provide an inspirational message for transforming our cities and our country.

Mayor Michael R. Turner
City of Dayton, OH

A silent church is a "saltless" church, and I firmly believe we should be involved in the global conversation—in subduing the earth and bringing it into subjection to the Kingdom of God. Bishop Marva Mitchell's book firmly grasps and puts forth the efficacy of a church full of salt and light. Her book demands that the 21st century belong to us…the Church!

Bishop Carlton D. Pearson
Presiding Bishop, Azusa Interdenominational Fellowship
Senior Pastor, Higher Dimensions Family Church
Tulsa, OK

Dr. Marva Mitchell is a very courageous warrior with a very courageous message. *It Takes a Church to Raise a Village* is a guttural battle cry wrung from the heart of someone who truly cares. In this treatise Marva dares to stride into the sick room of "coma Christianity" and shout forth offending truth. Poverty-stricken neighborhoods, drug-infested street corners, cruising gangs, inadequate schools, and filthy prisons are not going to be cured by government programs or social reform. Everyone is waiting for the Church to *wake up*. All of us should stop our religious routine just long enough to read this book.

Dr. Mark Hanby
Mark Hanby Ministries
CEO, Kingdom Vision Network

Dr. Mitchell's new book is awesome! As a model for faith-based ministry, this book is filled with practical Kingdom principles and precepts that work. This book is written for pastors, ministry leaders, politicians, and business leaders who want their ministry or area of responsibility to make a difference in the new millennium. Read this book and apply its truths, and a new power will be released to transform your church, community, city, suburb, and region.

It's time to lead, and this book teaches us how to lead effectively. Let's take back what belongs to the Kingdom and people of God right now.

Dr. Frank M. Reid III
Senior Pastor, Bethel A.M.E. Church
Baltimore, MD

Contents

Preface

It is said that the most important component of nation building is the family unit. In essence, the quality and state of the family determine the quality and state of a society and consequently the nation. This concept is not only true but has been proven by history, and can be identified as the source of most of our social ills today throughout the world. As goes the family, so goes the nation. The equation is simple—many families make up a community; many communities make up a society; and many societies make up a nation. Therefore, the quality of the family is the quality of the nation.

In this book, *It Takes a Church to Raise a Village*, Dr. Marva Mitchell takes us one step further and lays down a challenge to the Church to take responsibility for the nation. I strongly agree with her perspective, as I am of the persuasion that Jesus, in pronouncing the Great Commission to His Church, established an important mandate. He left the nation, not in the hands of the government, the scientists, the lawyers or the economists, but rather in the hands of the Church. He said, "Go into all the world and make disciples of every nation...teaching them everything I have taught you" (see Mt. 28:19-20; Mk. 16:15). This command places the responsibility of the nation squarely on the shoulders of the Church. The escapism theology of the twentieth-century Church, that pre-occupied itself with escaping to Heaven rather than impacting and changing the earth, has made the Church an irrelevant entity that is more an object of contempt than salvation for the world.

In this refreshing book, Dr. Mitchell refocuses our duty in the place where it belongs—the world. In her simple yet pro-found way she leaps over complicated theological concepts and serves up a practical directive that any believer or church group can apply immediately. I highly recommend this book to the serious student of the Word and to the disillusioned believer who knows that there is more to the Christian life than just waiting to go to Heaven.

I encourage you to read this book and embrace its princi-ples and precepts, because they are biblically sound and prac-tical. Let's take our responsibility. Let the Church rise up and embrace the mandate to raise the village in the way God intended.

Dr. Myles Munroe
Bahamas Faith Ministries
Nassau, Bahamas

Foreword

In the grand scheme of God's design, the limitation of those who fail to seek His will becomes clearer as time passes. Today we see the world, in failed attempt after failed attempt, trying to heal itself through schemes and programs that never touch the heart of the matter. The world's way lacks eternal moral foundations and generational significance. At the center of the issues is the disintegration of what we know as the family and the associated fallout on our children.

I am reminded of Colin Powell as he considered running for President of the United States. He and his wife, Alma, were addressing a group of urban elementary school students. The discussion was about family and the importance of those relationships, etc. A child raised her hand and innocently asked, "What is a family?" This is the state of our society. If we are not diligent, we are quickly approaching the day when the concept of family (a father married to a mother and living with children under one roof) will be a museum display.

World leaders quote the African proverb, "It takes a village to raise a child." However, a messed-up, immoral, out-of-focus village will produce children after its kind. This is what we see today. My dilemma is "Who is responsible for the restoration and nurturing of the village?" I firmly believe that this is the Church's responsibility as an agent of the Kingdom of God.

For too long, we have failed to live up to our calling in Christ to be *salt* and *light*. As God's children, we are to be living witnesses and examples of God's love and power, through Jesus Christ. The Bible says, "When the enemy comes in like a flood, the Spirit of the Lord will lift up a standard against him" (Is. 59:19b, NKJV). We are to be that standard of God. We cannot be effective if we do not go out to the flood. We fail when we go without God's Spirit and no one can see any difference between us and the world.

In the midst of a society of hurting children crying out for help, Dr. Mitchell challenges us all to look at ourselves. She confronts us with what we do in church as opposed to what we are called to be as the Church. We must address these issues! After all, the stakes are very high...our calling...our future...our destiny...our children.

Bishop Eddie L. Long, D.D., D.H.L.
Senior Pastor, New Birth Missionary Baptist Church
Lithonia, GA

Opportunities to serve people of impoverished and weakened conditions will come to us every day. The cup of cold water we'll have always ready, for our vision of Kingdom realities will make us much more sensitive to occasions to help and give. It may also lead us to make a point of discovering need, rather than always waiting for it to be thrust upon us.

Dallas Willard
American author

Introduction

An old African proverb asserts, "It takes a village to raise a child." In that village the child entered a society of order, experienced the comfort of its security, and learned the power of its established morality. The village provided leadership founded in integrity and exercised with moral character. In that cultural setting, R-E-S-P-E-C-T was more than a pop song—it was an expected way of life. When the village was in order, it was able to raise talented and stable children who reflected the values of the village.

In Hillary Clinton's book, *It Takes a Village*, she clearly characterizes some of the conditions of a village capable of raising children in a positive environment. She accurately insists that no family is an island and states, "...the society is our context; we do not exist in a vacuum."[1] The environment that our children grow up in leaves its marks on their future lives. Therefore, the condition of the village plays a fundamental part in their spiritual and social development.

Unfortunately, over the last few generations we have watched the gradual deterioration of our precious village. With much pain and grief we must all agree that the village in which we live is in deep need of major renovation—physically, socially, economically, and spiritually.

Where are the true role models for these desperate kids? Society's leaders are perceived as only concerned about their own political agendas, and their moral values are suspect. Entertainers and sports figures have emerged as the cultural "pop" heroes of this new generation, but the message they deliver is confused, materialistic, selfish, and often violent. Pornography pours into our homes through the television and the Internet, tearing at the moral fiber of the village wall. These deteriorating conditions have resulted in a further breaking down of the family and a general disrespect for life. Regrettably, the village has abandoned the children, leaving them unsupervised and hopelessly alone.

The words of Hans Kung, the German theologian, ring hauntingly true:

> "We may recall the problems of education. Educational programs, educational methods, educational goals and educational personnel are involved today in a far-reaching crisis. Educational authorities and those responsible for socialization (family, school, university, but also institutions and businesses) and likewise educational personnel (father, mother, teacher, educator, instructor) find that they are exposed to harsh criticism and impatient accusations from right and left: for some they are too conservative, for others too progressive; for some too political, for others too unpolitical; for some too authoritarian, for others too anti-authoritarian. Perplexity and disorientation are widespread. We can only outline the causes and conditions, symptoms and consequences of this crisis.

Introduction

"In the family: the acceleration of the rate of change in society means that parents not only grow older but often quickly lose touch with the situation. The criteria for educating their children are no longer certain. The result is a lack of understanding and knowledge. There is a profound insecurity which often leads to insistence on the wrong things and thus to disastrous conflicts of authority for children and family.

"In school and university: the discrepancy between pretension and reality, between often unrealistic theory and heightened practical expectations and requirements, the conflict of roles between teachers and pupils, professors and students, turn school and university into objects of political-educational controversy between all socially relevant groups and a field of experiment for more and more new educational-didactic projects and plans of study. After a planning euphoria we are now threatened with a planning lethargy, after excessive organization we are faced with disorganization, after the optimism of a future equality of opportunity we are uncertain about the future as a result of increasing restriction of studies; after conjuring up an educational emergency and the exhaustion of the last educational reserves we now have an educational glut and the 'academic proletariat.'

"And the young people themselves? At the center of the conflicts and contradictions of the educational scene, they are reacting increasingly with apathy, indifference and weariness and often enough break down completely. Taken seriously by society as consumers and pampered in their self-awareness also as consumers, at home and in school they are often made to feel irresponsible and dependent. Influenced by adults, by school attendance and the continual raising of the school-leaving age to think in terms of social prestige, they must see how dubious are the criteria of achievement, how remote from life their training has often been, and how uncertain are their future chances of an occupation.

"And the adults? Educational virtues, absolutely sacred and unquestioned yesterday, have apparently become obsolete today: adult authority, obedience to older people, subordination to the parents' will, adaptation to the existing order. But now there are some who question not only the contents and methods but the very idea of education. Those who identified education with determination by others, manipulation, imposition of the teacher's will, now go to the other extreme and advocate anti-authoritarian education, absolute self-determination, unrestricted freedom; aggression is to be cultivated, frustrations worked out, instincts satisfied, conflicts encouraged. Relationships are reversed: young people are no longer subject to the will of adults, but the claims of adults are subordinated to the claims, needs and requirements of young people."[2]

The village is no longer qualified or adequately prepared to raise a child because the village itself must be raised. How can the village be rescued? Who or what will it take to raise the village? There can only be one answer to this question: *It Takes a Church to Raise a Village!*

If the Church is to raise the village, it must stop *having* church and start *being* the Church. We can no longer have church as usual. The Church must come out from behind its walls and begin to impact the village through a display of the love of Christ and a demonstration of the power of Christ.

Introduction

Inside our walled fortresses we have carried out our religious exercises—singing our songs, praying our prayers, preaching our sermons, giving our money—while the village lies in ruins all around us.

Church, this is our day! We must rise up and take responsibility for the village. The government alone is unable to save the village. They are now turning to the Church for help, and the Church must take this responsibility. At the same time the Church must turn to her Lord for a new empowerment and a fresh filling of His love. It is the Church who is called to be light to the world. It is the Church who must set the godly example. It is the Church who must establish integrity and biblical standards. The Church possesses the wisdom and power to raise the village and set a new course for the future. Now the Church must rise up and shake off the collected dust of indifference and inadequacy to face the challenges that are before us.

The Bible says, "Where sin abounded, grace did much more abound" (Rom. 5:20b). The power and penalty of sin has raised its hideous head in our village. That head must be cut off cleanly and decisively by a compassionate demonstration of God's grace. Grace is not a theological thought; it is a vibrant reality exhibited in loving acts of mercy and expressed through the empowering presence of the Lord. We must arise as administrators of the grace of God and become practitioners of the Word of God.

There are more opportunities for the Church than ever before. Congress has passed laws, such as "The Personal Responsibility and Work Opportunity Reconciliation Act of 1996," to release churches to interact with the community. This bipartisan act includes a "Charitable Choice" provision, affording the opportunity for government funding to be received by churches and other religious groups, to help lift families out of poverty. We have no excuse to stay in our comfort zones.

A cloud of misery and apathy overshadows the village surrounding the Church. Our youth are referred to as "Generation X" and labeled as predators. They are stuck in a slough of despair and are powerless to move toward their predestined potential. The Church needs to become a distributor of hope in Jesus Christ. We hold the keys to their destiny, and it is time to unlock the prison doors and let the village prisoners free. It is only the Rock of Christ that can provide a solid place upon which to stand when all other ground is sinking sand.

Isaiah 61:1-3 states,

> *The Spirit of the Lord God is upon me; because the Lord hath anointed me to preach good tidings unto the meek; He hath sent me to bind up the brokenhearted, to proclaim liberty to the captives, and the opening of the prison to them that are bound; to proclaim the acceptable year of the Lord, and the day of vengeance of our God; to comfort all that mourn; to appoint unto them that mourn in Zion, to give unto them beauty for ashes, the oil of joy for mourning, the garment of praise for the spirit of heaviness; that they might be called trees of righteousness, the planting of the Lord, that He might be glorified.*

The village is filled with the oppressed and brokenhearted. A spirit of heaviness pervades the cultural atmosphere. Too many sit at the frightful edges of our religious reach untouched by the love of our living Lord. Now is the time to stand up and extend our hands to these victims, lifting them up into the loving arms of the Lord who can heal them and give them a living hope. Are we prepared to bind up the brokenhearted, loose the captives, cover the naked, and drive off the spirit of heaviness with shouts of glorious praise? We are filled with the Spirit of God and now must release our compassion

Introduction

and anointing on these disenfranchised ones. Let's position ourselves to raising the standard of life in the village rather than maintaining our religious status quo. We have a mandate to touch the world beginning with our own village. We cannot expect others, such as financial corporations, social agencies, or government institutions, to do it. *It Takes a Church to Raise a Village!*

The Church has been given the greatest opportunity since the writing of the Book of Acts to significantly alter the state of the village. Our tools for renovation are the love of Christ, the truth of the gospel, and the power of the Spirit. A divine summons has been issued from Heaven. Angelic forces have arrived at the door of the Church urging us to respond quickly. We are being compelled by the Spirit of God to give a dream to the destitute, to provide new desires for the downtrodden, and to deliver a stimulus to the skeptical and a purpose to the pariah of society.

What a glorious day for the Church! We must seize this moment. This is our day to raise the village. It's time to become a spring in the desert and stop preaching to the choir. It's time to die to ourselves that others might be raised up in newness of life.

Let's put aside our doctrinal differences and selfish schemes and agree that Jesus is the answer. The village is dying while we are debating. We spend too much time tearing each other apart when we should be putting the village back together. Our strength is our unity, and it is the great passion of the Lord that we be one. We are all the Body of Christ and together we are forged into a formidable force that cannot be resisted. We must begin to walk out our faith and believe that we can make a difference in turning the village around.

My purpose in this book is to stir up your compassion and commitment. I want to move the Church into the mission field of the village. This book is not intended to be a put-down but a get-up for the Church, who has the ability to halt and reverse the decay of the village. Are we ready to say, "Enough is enough"? Are we ready to come out of hiding and become ambassadors for the gospel? Let us move forward in the confident understanding that:

It Takes a Church to Raise a Village!

Endnotes

1. Hillary Rodham Clinton, *It Takes a Village* (New York: Simon & Schuster, 1996), 32.

2. From *On Being a Christian* by Hans Kung, copyright © 1976 by Doubleday, a division of Bantam Doubleday Dell Publishing Group, Inc. Used by permission of Doubleday, a division of Random House, Inc.

Chapter One

Temperament lies behind mood: behind will, lies the fate of character. Then behind both, the influence of family the tyranny of culture: and finally the power of climate and environment; and we are free, only to the extent we rise above these.

John Burroughs (1837-1921)
U.S. author, naturalist

Chapter One

Building the Waste Places

And they that shall be of thee shall build the old waste places: thou shalt raise up the foundations of many generations; and thou shalt be called, The repairer of the breach, The restorer of paths to dwell in (Isaiah 58:12).

Sacred Cows and Whited Sepulchres

Since I was a small child I had dreamed of visiting the Taj Mahal. The magnificence of this stately structure had captured my imagination early in life and had magnetic powers that drew me with an irresistible force. My chance to see it with my own eyes had finally come as I sat on the plane en route to my first ministry trip to India. My thoughts were rushing ahead with wild expectation as I anticipated the trip to this amazing man-made wonder.

My son and I arrived at the hotel, physically exhausted and anxious to get to our rooms. As we waited at the desk we were greeted with the unbelievable news that our reservations had been canceled because of a convention in town. We stood there in shock and dismay as we contemplated the alternatives. We were then directed to another hotel that was of much lesser quality. We finally arrived at our new destination and immediately checked in to the hotel.

Eager to get some rest, we made our way to our rooms. As I opened the door to my room, a lizard scurrying across the floor greeted me. Needless to say, this little creature was not

5

my idea of an acceptable roommate, so I quickly requested another room. The next room looked as though it had not been cleaned for a month, but I was too tired to make any more fuss. Finally, I was able to get my things unpacked, and I settled down for a few hours of sleep before we made our trek to the Taj Mahal.

After a short nap, my son Willie and I hurried to catch a train for the four-hour ride. Bear in mind that this was not the Amtrak—spacious and luxurious. This was an Indian train crowded with hundreds of people determinedly and inconsiderately pushing their way on and off at each stop where only a few minutes were allotted for passengers to get on board or disembark. No one seemed to care that I was walking with a cane. It appeared their only concern was that if they missed this train, they would have to wait four or five hours for the next one. As Willie and I pushed ourselves into the middle of the crowd moving en masse towards the train, we eventually got on board.

After the hectic and exhausting ride, we arrived worn out but excited, anticipating the final reward of our journey. I was eager to get off the train to avoid the mass exodus, and jumped out of my seat as quickly as I could. Shocked as I flew by him and concerned that I might injure myself, Willie quickly reached out to assist me.

With dogged determination I pushed my way through the train station, past the mass of crippled and afflicted people. Everywhere I looked I was confronted with poverty and pain. With empty and shriveled hands, they reached out begging for whatever I might give them. We just couldn't stop if we were to meet the driver waiting to take us to our destination. I knew if I stopped to help even one person, I would quickly drown in a sea of desperate beggars.

Building the Waste Places

At last we reached our driver and drove off in the direction of the historic site. The cab ride to the Taj Mahal was a real adventure. Our driver started our journey with an endless stream of stories, detailing his poverty and desperate needs. However, the cloud of despair and destitution that his stories created was soon cut short. Along the way, as though it was strategically planned, he took us to store after store for the purpose of shopping. We disturbingly discovered that these shops were owned by this cunning cab driver. We knew that we were dealing with a real con artist, but more importantly he knew where we wanted to go and how to get us there.

In spite of his devious ways, this colorful individual did keep us laughing with his descriptions of life in India. At one point we nearly ran into a large cow that had crossed our path. Our driver slowed down as we carefully drove by this "sacred" animal. The cab trip taught us much about driving in this land and the need to be alert to all kind of revered obstacles and dangerous turns. Our driver explained that in India you needed to have good brakes, great reaction time, and most of all, good luck. Riding with this man convinced me that what we really needed was Jesus.

At last we arrived safely at the gate to the Taj Mahal. Our driver stopped the car and informed us that we would have to walk the last half-mile to the site. We paid our driver his fee and watched as he drove off in the distance. As we turned around, our eyes were greeted with a glorious view of the Taj Mahal far in the distance. I'll never forget my first sight of the shimmering brilliance that resplendently reflected off the white marble dome. It rose majestically and mysteriously out of the distant mist—a teardrop on the cheek of time, as the Indian poet Tagore described it.

With my physical disability, I knew it would be very difficult to walk that distance, but I was determined to reach my lifelong goal. My son began to set up my wheelchair, but I was in no mood to wait. I started to walk as fast as I could toward the celebrated shrine. Willie shouted, "Mom, sit down in your chair." I replied, "Catch me if you can." Later as I thought about that incident, I was reminded of how many times God has a place of rest for us, but we choose to move on in our own disabled condition.

Willie finally caught up with me and literally scooped me up into the wheelchair for the final leg of our journey. I could hardly contain my excitement. I was so thrilled and focused on getting to the Taj Mahal that I hardly noticed we were being charged a fee to enter the grounds, nor did I mind having my purse searched and my candy and chewing gum removed. *Take whatever you want*, I thought, *I'm here now.*

As we arrived at a large gate, we entered through a massive portal leading into a magnificent fortress. As one stands inside the main gate of the Taj Mahal, his eyes are directed to an arch that frames it.

The Taj Mahal rises on a high red sandstone base topped by a huge white marble terrace on which rests the famous dome flanked by four tapering minarets. As I stood there in total awe, the view overtook all my senses and left me absolutely breathless. With my mouth hanging open and my heart beating faster, I stood there thunderstruck in the presence of this architectural marvel. Apparently, it is common for tourists to be awestruck by the first sighting because guards stationed at the gateway literally push people along so that the gateway is not clogged with pilgrims overwhelmed by the sight.

The splendor of this brilliant masterpiece filled the totality of my vision. I was quickly drawn to the luminous radiance of the dome that gently swelled so high above this massive structure, majestically positioned at the top. As my eyes traveled downward, the beauty of the pure white marble decorated with gold and precious stones arrested my attention. I stood there paralyzed by the beauty all around me. I forced myself to take my eyes off this glorious edifice and look at the surrounding environs that decorated the royal grounds of the Taj Mahal. There were elegantly decorated gardens and sparkling crystal pools that spread around the building. At each corner were towers clearly defined by the four domes reaching upward toward the sky. I was staggered by the magic and magnetism of the transcendent beauty of this imperial place.

It was time for us to make our way inside. When we arrived at the doorway to the main structure, we were required to take off our shoes so as not to scuff or wear down the precious marble floors, where millions of feet have crossed. I was unable to remove my shoes because of my physical challenge, so they gave me special coverings for my feet. You can imagine how dangerous it was as I walked cautiously across the very slippery marble surface.

What I saw inside the monument was almost beyond description. I was moving towards a state of high ecstasy as each new scene crashed into an already overloaded sensory system. I was overwhelmed by the image of the gleaming marble walls richly embellished with precious gemstones inlaid in intricate patterns. I gently reached out to touch those marble walls rubbing my hands over their cool smooth surface. I marveled at the creative triumph of the man that constructed such magnificent splendor. How was it that the builders of this monument could stay so focused on its completion for 12 years regardless of the cost in lives and resources? This was truly an amazing feat of creative genius and steadfast resolution.

Soon we were approaching the end of the day and I waited to see what many had told me would be the most glorious sight. As the sun began its descent towards the horizon, its powerful bands of light appeared to change the very color and appearance of the majestic monument. The structure transformed right before my very eyes. It appeared as though the Taj Mahal had a life of its own. The rays of light pounded on the precious stones and reflecting pools as they gathered up and intensified every color of the regal towers, the marbled construction, and the imposing dome high above all.

During the day I had noticed pigeons flying around the monument; but as evening approached, they settled down and actually vanished from our sight. In a dramatic display of natural contrast, powerful eagles replaced the presence of the pigeons.

I eventually found a bench and sat down for a while, quietly reliving the spectacular events of the day. I lifted up my head to get one long-lasting look and to take one final picture. Who would ever believe that "me," a little black girl from the 'hood, was sitting where Princess Diana had once sat to be photographed? That moment is one that is permanently fixed in my memory.

As I turned to walk away from the grandeur and majesty of the Taj Mahal, another spectacle far less beautiful took shape right before my eyes.

A small child approached me and began pulling on my jacket. She was evidently a frequent visitor to the site. Her frail tug drew me back from the majesty all around me. The daunting eyes of this little beggar penetrated deeply into my heart. She was not alone. As I looked around, I saw many more just like her—filthy faces, malnourished, and scantily clothed. Surrounding the stately beauty of the Taj Mahal was a horrible exhibition of incredible poverty and suffering. Suddenly the excitement of the day lost its grip on me and began to fade into the recesses of my mind. The landscape of poverty and despair was begging for my attention and crying out for a response.

As my soul quivered with the shock of the depressing deprivation all around me, I heard the voice of the Lord beginning to speak. He transformed this dramatic scene into a spiritual vision of the destitute state of the Church. The Lord had brought me to the other side of the world so that He could powerfully demonstrate what was happening in our own backyard.

Self-created Walls

We have been so focused on the form and fanfare in the Church that we have failed to see and speak to the wastelands that are at our border's edge. We are so engaged in the things that we are building that we have neglected the needs of the village wasteland.

In spite of its extravagant stateliness, the Taj Mahal is merely a white marble tomb, empty and cold. It reminds one of the "whited sepulchres" that Jesus spoke of in Matthew 23:27, referring to religious men who observed the laws of religion while disregarding the heart of religion, the gospel of Jesus Christ that brings hope to those in despair.

The Church should be a sanctuary of life for the village, not a stronghold that excludes them from the life of God. We have put forth our own "sacred cows" of religion that have become great stumbling blocks for those outside our carefully constructed boundaries. We are more concerned with maintaining the elegance of our edifices than ministering to the plight of people all around us. We are so hectic in *having church* that we fail in *being the Church*.

The Church continues to expand the borders of her premises with larger structures that promote pious agendas. Like the poverty that surrounds the Taj Mahal, the villages around our beautiful churches lie in ruins. Our schools are war zones, while outside their fenced facilities are families devastated by destitution, dysfunctionalism, and despair. The gangs in the village destroy the lives of her youth with drive-by shootings, while the Church just drives by, oblivious to those lying wasted in the streets.

In the same way that I walked right through the poverty that surrounded the Taj Mahal, the Church drives through the village neighborhoods, hoping the traffic light does not turn red, nervously locking their car doors, and rolling up windows with cell phones in their hands.

The Church lives in fear of the village surrounding them. They are more concerned about the village *breaking in* to their beautiful facilities than about *breaking out* into the neighborhood with the power of the glorious gospel of our Lord.

The Church must move beyond her self-created walls and rebuild the waste places.

Rebuilding the Waste Places

How shall we describe these waste places? They are the cities and neighborhoods in which we live. They are abandoned buildings and deserted businesses, vacant lots, crumbling government housing projects, and graffiti-covered buildings run by slumlords. This desolation has created a people who are paralyzed with fear, overcome with hopelessness, and overrun with abandoned kids and neglected teens.

The government is not the longed-for Messiah. They have poured money into depressed neighborhoods and distressed communities, yet the problems of the village remain. Until we change the heart of the hopeless, we will never be able to permanently change the state of their surroundings.

The love of Christ can energize the Church and give her motivation for reconstructing the waste places. By manifesting the love of Christ to the village, the Church has the power to change hearts. We can be the extension of Christ's hand, reaching out to touch the lives of hopeless children one heart at a time. We have the resources to rebuild the waste places and are under divine obligation to start the work immediately. It's time to get up off our knees and roll up our sleeves.

The Foundations

The starting place for all reconstruction is rebuilding the foundation. The foundation of the village has always been the family structure. Families mean generations. If we are going to change the family, we must reach out to every member of the family. In order to help the life of the village, the Church must get involved in family dynamics. The Church must become a place of instruction where parents are taught how to train their children in biblical truth and lead them into spiritual reality.

Dumbfounded by Divorce

My heart breaks as I read of the deterioration of the American family. This disease has broken out in the Church as well. The rates of divorce among those in the Church are three percent higher than that of the surrounding village. In a recent article published in the *Dallas Morning News* entitled "Dumbfounded by Divorce," the Barna Research Group raised the proverbial eyebrow by its finding that "born-again Christians" are more likely to divorce than atheists. The study goes on to show that 34 percent of the members of non-denominational churches went through divorce as opposed to 27 percent of the general population. Jews had a divorce rate of 30 percent, "born-again Christians" 27 percent, Evangelical Christians 25 percent, Mormons 24 percent and atheist/agnostics 21 percent. These statistics are not given to embarrass and hurt those who have had to endure the pain of divorce. We simply point out that this problem is prevalent throughout all strata of society.

Mormons who have been married in the temple have an uncommonly low divorce rate. Mormons are quick to declare that the success of their marriages is due to strict church requirements for marriage and the character of the people who are challenged to meet them. Mormons date within their own faith and are married with their sights set on having a family. They are committed to their faith and attend church regularly. The Mormon wedding ceremony is sacred and only attended by close friends, family, and those in faithful church attendance.

> *If we can create a pathway for the power of God to flow into the village family, we can become the agents of healing and health.*

Whenever they have marital difficulty, they are more likely to seek help from the spiritual support that surrounds them. They take responsibility for the training of their children and for creating happy, stable marriages. They have "family home evenings" instead of Monday Night Football, which establishes bonds between family members and makes the marriage stronger. While we do not agree with the theology and practice of the Mormons, we are impressed with the strength of their families.

These are challenging times with so many forces warring against the family. But three words that will make marriage work are *prayer*, *prayer*, and *prayer*. If we can create a pathway for the power of God to flow into the village family, we can become the agents of healing and health. However, we must give them more than words. We must model the message. As we, the Bride of Christ, model the message of the Bridegroom, there will be hope for the family in the village.

Family Violence

One of the major causes for the breakdown in the family is violence. A woman is beaten every 15 seconds. Domestic violence is the leading cause of injury to women between the ages of 15 and 44 in the United States. It is sad reality that this nation has more animal shelters than it does women shelters. Battered women are more likely to suffer miscarriages or have children with birth defects.

One-third of the children who witness the battering of their mothers will go on to manifest significant behavioral problems. These deviant behaviors include psychosomatic disorders, stuttering, anxiety, bed wetting, and sleeping disorders. Coupled with displaying psychological symptoms, these kids will also "act out" their hurt and pain in school. This is exhibited in failing grades, skipping classes, fighting, and rebelling against school authorities.

The nuclear family is living under a curse of dysfunctionalism, including parental abandonment, financial bondage, educational limitations, and hopeless despondency. But the most serious dysfunction in the family is the absence of Jesus Christ. The Church must step into this maze of anger and despair providing a way of escape to those caught in the web of family disorders. It is the Church who bears the responsibility to introduce Christ to the village family. The Church must restore the foundation of the village, which is the family.

Repairers of the Breach

There is a breach in the village. That breach is the great chasm that exists between our youth and the adults in the village. Our youth see adults as the enemy. They have turned their backs on their parents to pursue drugs, alcohol, sex, and violence. These are the demons that bid for their souls.

But the biggest breach is the gap that exists between the Church and the youth of the village. It is crucial that the Church extend their youth ministry beyond the walls of their buildings and reach into the neighborhoods that surround them. The challenge before them is to extend the love and compassion of Jesus to these "hurting ones."

As we reach out in love, we must be prepared to deal with rejection and bad language. Extend the same grace to them that God extends to you. We can repair the breach between the youth and the Church if we reach out to them in loving care. The youth of the Church can become a powerful tool in the hands of God for reaching lonely and desperate kids. The emphasis in our churches must change from entertaining church youth to equipping and empowering them to reach young people outside the church walls.

Young people are the most powerful agents for reform and change, and therefore, they are the main focus of the enemy. He always comes to steal the seed. We must provide a new direction for our youth. Isaiah 43:19-20 states:

> Behold, I will do a new thing; now it shall spring forth; shall ye not know it? I will even make a way in the wilderness, and rivers in the desert. The beast of the field shall honour Me, the dragons and the owls: because I give waters in the wilderness, and rivers in the desert, to give drink to My people, My chosen.

The most effective way to repair the breach is through the power of love and understanding. First Corinthians 13 is our road map and guide. We must allow our youth to remain youth. We must reach them and speak to them in the language they understand. We may not like the language they speak or the music they listen to, but if God chooses to reach them with Christian rap music, then we must learn to speak that language. We must make our faith relevant to them.

I remember when they told us in the Pentecostal church that TV was of the devil. The new devil for Pentecostal TV evangelists is the music of our youth. How things have changed! How did God reach you? What might your grandparents think of the music you use in worship today? We will only reach the village youth when we learn to communicate in their terms. Music is simply a form of communication, and we must learn how to communicate through the form that they have chosen.

Michal, the wife of David, criticized him for his method of praise. We should remember that it led to barrenness or unfruitfulness for the rest of her life. Her response to him is much the same as ours toward the music and worship our kids are using to worship God. Is it possible that we are jeopardizing our own fruitfulness when we criticize the way our youth worship God? It is true that God never changes, but His methods do. If we don't open our hearts and change our methods, we run the risk of losing another generation.

There are 617 juvenile detention centers in the United States, and the demand for more is rising. However, warehousing the stolen seed of the next generation is not the answer. The Church has the power and ability to bring them in from off the streets and show them that they are loved and possess great value. God has given us the tools to repair the breaches. If we pick up these tools, we can prevent the need for more rehabilitation centers. Are we willing to stop *having* church long enough to bring them into the Kingdom?

Restorers of the Path

Along with the breakdown in the family and the despair of our youth is another problem. The village has no standard by which to live. Our society is floating on vacillating values and drifting dogmas.

Proverbs 22:6 tells us to "train up a child in the way he should go: and when he is old, he will not depart from it."

But how shall we train them and where shall we lead them? We, the Church, should train them in the Word of God and lead them to the Shepherd of the flock.

It Takes a Church to Raise a Village

I consider myself somewhat of an expert on raising children having been blessed with seven of them myself. Because my husband and I raised seven children who were very close in age, we made great sacrifices to make sure they received what they needed. At one point I owned only one dress that I wore to church every Sunday so that my children would look presentable. Today, because I was willing to pay the price, all seven of my children are working in the ministry of the Lord.

In the years of raising my own children, I learned a few secrets. One key secret is that children learn more by what we do than by what we say. Our values and standards are better established by the life that we live as opposed to the words that we speak. We have much to give them, and they will be only too happy to accept what we have if it is given through a heart of love and by a life of reality.

I recall a visit to a village in Kenya. While I was watching some children playing in the dirt, I decided I wanted to give them something. I spotted a small market and went to purchase some candy for the children. When I first offered the candy, the children approached me with caution; but once the treats were in their hands, they immediately became more comfortable with me. I was so focused on what I was doing, I did not notice that I had attracted an entire village of children whose hands were outstretched to receive the gift. This simple illustration demonstrates how quickly our kids are ready to receive.

Church, are you willing to risk being run over by the children of the village? What has God placed in your hands that might be attractive to them? If we are to restore the path for our children, we must be willing to do what it takes to arrest their attention. It might mean that we have to sacrifice our nice carpets and beautiful facilities to bring them in. If you are going to invite the children of the village into your home, your carpet will get dirty. How committed are we to lifting these kids out of their maze of misery? In a sense the children are our own pathways to the future. If we ignore the children of the village, we do so at the cost of our very future.

A Gathering of Eagles

Those powerful eagles that replaced the pigeons at the Taj Mahal were not content to simply graze on the grounds all day long. Their great passion was to soar far above those grounds. The Lord has shown me that He is replacing the leadership and spirit of the Church. Just as the eagle has vision many times that of man, we must look beyond mere human perception and expectation for the Church and her role in restoring the village. To be sure, there will be obstacles, trials, and storms. But the eagle can fly into the face of the storm without fear. Rather than being a pigeon roosting at sunset, we are to be a gathering of eagles establishing the rule of God over the village as it is rebuilt, repaired, and restored.

It Takes a Church to Raise a Village!

Chapter Two

The test of the morality of a society is what it does for its children.

Dietrich Bonhoeffer
German theologian

Chapter Two

Can You Hear Them Crying?

And I will rejoice in Jerusalem, and joy in My people: and the voice of weeping shall be no more heard in her, nor the voice of crying (Isaiah 65:19).

One night as my husband and I were preparing for bed, the telephone rang. The voice at the other end of the telephone was crying out hysterically and incoherently. I could not understand a single word she was saying. I desperately tried to calm her so I could make sense out of her frantic cries. Suddenly, a scream pierced my heart, "They shot Toby!" Stunned, I couldn't believe what I was hearing. I asked her to repeat it again hoping I had misunderstood her frenzied words. The answer was the same. "They shot Toby! He's dead! A drug dealer shot him!" My heart sank and my knees weakened as I fell onto the bed next to my husband. I dropped the phone as I repeated to him the tragic news. Lorraine's son Toby had been shot and killed. Lorraine was my best friend and it was her mother, Toby's grandmother, who had made the call. I picked up the phone again and assured her I was on the way.

I had no idea that a small drug war was being fought in our community, and now someone we knew personally had become a casualty of that meaningless conflict. Arriving at the home, I could see the bullet holes in the car in which Toby had been killed. I was shocked and grieved at this senseless crime of revenge that had been aimed at Toby's brother, the result of

25

a drug deal gone bad. Toby was an innocent and uninvolved victim. He had been an honor student on his way to a bright future at Ohio State to play football. He was cut down in a horrible fashion in the very prime of his life.

Toby's grandmother asked me to go to Lorraine's place of employment, where she was working third shift as a private duty nurse, and tell her what had happened to her son. The ride to deliver this appalling news was a ten-mile trip of tears. As a reluctant messenger, I prepared myself to convey the worst kind of news.

I can't begin to describe my feelings as I approached the door where Lorraine was working. What words could I possibly say? I hesitated there at the door. My message was going to bring grief beyond imagination to my precious friend and turn her world upside down. I didn't want to deliver this grievous blow, but I could not delay any longer. As Lorraine opened the door and saw my face, she knew something was terribly wrong. I embraced her and whispered in her ear that Toby had been shot and killed. As the words penetrated into her deepest being, she collapsed in my arms and began to weep uncontrollably. We held each other as I attempted to absorb her grief into my own soul. When the crying had finally subsided, I sent her home to comfort her grieving children. Because I was also a private duty nurse, I finished her shift for her.

When I returned home the next morning, I found my husband on his knees praying. As he was getting up, he told me that he had asked the Lord, "Where is the Church?" The Lord responded with a swift and penetrating answer. "*You* are the Church." His life was forever changed by that word. From that day until his last, he was devoted to reaching the young men of the city with the hope of the gospel.

The Sound of Crying

There is a sound of crying in the village. It is the sound of crying mothers at funerals for their children lost to drugs and violence. There is a tragic cry from abortion clinics as young girls have the life of a child sucked out of them because they feel they have no other choice. Listen to the heartrending cry lifted up from the halls of Columbine and other schools where students have lost their lives at the hands of a lonely or disgruntled peer. There is a hopeless cry rising from our nation's courtrooms where guilty verdicts strip freedom from young men and women who then disappear behind walls of incarceration, leaving behind families and friends. There is the despondent cry from nursing homes that house our discarded elderly. Who can ignore the cries of tired grandparents who raise their children's children because the parents are strung out on crack and alcohol? There are too many cries coming from children who have no food. How can a country who feeds the world allow their own children to go to bed hungry? As I have asked my congregation many times, *"Can you hear them crying?"*

Beginning to Hush the Cry

My husband and I first heard the cries years ago. In 1989 we became aware of the many inner-city children who went without meals on the weekends. Most of their weekly meals were a result of government-funded school breakfast and lunch programs. These children were anxious to go to school on Monday mornings just so they could fill their empty bellies. We began driving our bus into the projects on the weekends, knocking on doors, and inviting children to the church to become a part of what we called our "Love School." The children were received by loving volunteers who fed them with food and the Word of God.

It Takes a Church to Raise a Village

After only a few Saturdays had passed, a teacher stopped me in the hallway confessing that she was having a difficult time teaching Bible lessons to the children because many of them could not read. After visiting the classrooms, I found that the teacher's description was accurate. I decided that something must be done so I called all the teachers together, collected the Bibles, and sent them to the Learning Education Store to buy reading materials. Almost by accident, we started a literacy program—a program that developed into one that would eventually earn awards at the state and national levels. Our Saturday program was geared to not only help the children, but the whole family as well.

Our success with the children in the Love School convinced us that we could do even more. I called the superintendent of schools, the chief of police, and the mayor's office and asked to meet with them. We next wanted to provide an alternative for students from ages 6 to 16 who had been suspended from school. Our desire was to create a structured environment for these students in order to keep them off the streets and supervise their schoolwork. As we sat around the conference table, I could almost see them rolling their eyes as if to say, "Here's another church wanting to do something but will never follow through." But we did what we promised and even more.

When we started the program, we had no financial support. Soon, however, various groups were made aware of our efforts. The United Way called and offered to help us fill out papers so that we could receive a grant as a reading specialist. Besides that they gave us a grant of $37,000. We also received many donations in the form of cash and computers. The dream was becoming a reality.

Our programs now serve most of the schools in Dayton and many of the schools in Montgomery County, Ohio. We also have a work study suspension program where students receive tutoring and counseling sessions. To help them develop a strong work ethic, we help them get involved in various community services. We have since changed the name of the program to STAND (Students Taking A New Direction). The program has yielded dramatic results in students' behavior, attitudes, and success in the classroom.

We heard the sound of crying and responded with a conscious decision to hush that cry with the powerful declaration of the gospel of hope.

Let's take a closer look at a few areas where I believe the Church can bring the healing love of Jesus Christ and stop the weeping in the village.

Cries From the Schools

There are cries coming from our nation's schools. The schools in our village used to be a safe and secure haven for our children. In my day, the worst that happened was a bloody nose from a fight, usually broken up by a hall monitor. Where do these cries now come from and why doesn't anyone listen?

In 1996, there were more than 255,000 acts of violence including some horrible devastating murders that took place on school property. Why has there been such escalation in school violence? I believe we have not applied the blood of Christ over the doorposts of the schoolhouse and the angel of death is killing our children. Marijuana, cocaine, crack, and other drugs are being sold right on our school grounds. The presence of gangs has increased and nearly doubled in some inner-city schools, increasing the likelihood of more death and violence. One study claimed that as many as 270,000 students carry weapons to school every day. Why? Children from devastated families are reaching out to anyone who will give them a sense of belonging and identity. They carry weapons to make them feel safe and important. How much have we attempted to reverse the curse that is upon our local schools? Are we too busy with Sunday school that we have forgotten and neglected the village schools? We must make the village school a priority—a prize. How many will die before we share the spiritual antidote for the poison of violence in our schools? The life of Christ is the only hope for reversing this hideous trend.

The religious folks of the Church react to this catastrophic condition by shaking their heads and saying, "If only they had not taken God and prayer out of the schools." This is a weak, feeble response to a grave situation. It is a callous answer given without much thought or insight into the complications of the plight that plagues our schools. The fact is, it is impossible to take either prayer or God out of the schools. This is simply a matter of our religious mind-set and attitude. We can pray anywhere and anytime we choose. No one can regulate a prayer offered up to God from the heart of one of His kids. Do you think that God abides by our ridiculous restrictions?

I prefer to convert a child before the crime than have to comfort a parent after the crime.

Have you noticed that when there is a tragedy, such as what happened at Columbine, the first people called are the pastors. There is never a shortage of prayer ascending to the Father *after* such tragedies. Our prayers are quickly received in times of trouble; but why can't we be more effective at preventing these tragedies? I prefer to convert a child before the crime than have to comfort a parent after the crime.

We must create pockets of prayer for our schools, lifting up students, teachers, administrators, schools board members, and all who are involved in our educational systems. We must reach out to the village children through our own empowered

30

youth by building relationships with individual students. Local churches can start programs like the Love School or STAND in their own village schools. Why not go to the principals of your local schools and offer your support in whatever way they suggest? Have you considered developing your own specialized programs such as after-school, drug prevention, and literacy programs? There is much that can be accomplished. The Church can do more than perform memorial services after the damage has already been done.

The cries from the village school have not subsided. Only the Church has the capacity to silence that cry. Only the Church has the ability to provide direction and offer hope for these youth who are disoriented and depressed. We must begin to pay attention.

Can you hear them crying?

Cries From the Abortion Clinics

There are soul-wrenching cries screaming at us from the abortion clinics. *Can you hear them crying?* Our country has legalized the murder of the unborn and we casually call it "pro-choice." The enemy always attacks the seed of the next generation. In ancient times, babies were tossed into the fire as bloody sacrifices to non-existent gods. In Moses' time, Pharaoh attempted to slaughter all the babies to keep a nation in bondage. In the time of our Lord, Herod murdered the innocent to assure the continuity of his kingly reign.

Matthew 2:18 says, "In Rama was there a voice heard, lamentation, and weeping, and great mourning, Rachel weeping for her children, and would not be comforted, because they are not."

Can you hear them crying?

Why would a young girl abandon her most sacred of responsibilities? Is it possible that she felt there was no other

31

alternative? Perhaps she got pregnant searching for the love and attention she could find in no other way. Maybe she had no family support and the father of her child wanted nothing to do with her. What began as a search for love has ended in the tragedy of death and a lifetime of regret.

Local churches have organized pro-life marches all over the country, spending millions of dollars campaigning against abortion. Sadly, we have not reduced the number of abortions, and the laws continue to support the right to kill the unborn. Is there no other alternative to save our seed?

Anyone can carry a sign protesting in front of an abortion clinic. It's easy—after our protest, there is no other accountability. We go home having done our religious duty and feel good that we got involved. But while we sit in our comfortable chairs considering our courageous actions, the problem continues to manifest its ugly head. They will continue to kill babies until we, the Church, respond in love and action. Since that time my husband asked the Lord that day on his knees, "Where is the Church?" the answer has remained the same: "*You* are the Church."

Does your church offer sex education? Do you support parents' ability to discuss these issues with their kids? Or are you living in the past where talking of sex is taboo? The youth of the congregations do talk about sex, and sometimes it happens in our sacred pews. It's time to deal with these issues directly from the pulpit. The Church will only be able to raise the village and end the crying at the abortion clinics when it faces reality and addresses the issue of sex. We need to begin to educate the youth of the village about sex rather than leaving it up to the public schools whose sole solution is to hand out condoms. We must move beyond careless and thoughtless preventative measures. We must instruct our kids in the dangers of pre-marital sex. The Church is responsible for raising the standard.

Churches should have adoption committees and classes about foster care parenting. We can become the extended family for the village. We live in larger homes with fewer people making more money to provide for smaller families. We must become a family to those suffering with unwanted pregnancies. The Bible says in Psalm 68:6, "God setteth the solitary in families...." The Church must extend her homes in mercy, not judgment to the teenage mother. Offer to assist her in developing parenting skills. Help her to develop skills that will enable her to find employment. The village outside the Church is unfortunately doing nothing to help her face these challenging circumstances. It is more convenient for our society to offer a death solution rather than a life solution.

It is just not enough for us to be on the right side of the cause for life. Having the right political and moral view is not a substitute for our own personal involvement in the lives of those who carry the seed of the next generation. There is a demonstration that will have lasting and practical value. It is the demonstration of the love of Jesus Christ in a loving involvement in the lives of these troubled young people. We need to put down the signs and pick up the babies.

Can you hear them crying?

Cries From the Prisons

There is a cry of despair escalating in intensity from our prison systems. Men and women are locked away in confinement that could last a lifetime. Too often in the village, precious children are left without fathers or mothers. They often shift from one foster care facility to another. The populations of prisons are growing at an alarming rate. It's obvious the government does not have the answer. They are discovering that all their attempts at rehabilitation have been a miserable failure. But because these prisons are filled to capacity, they continue to spend millions of dollars on building new ones. A wiser investment of those tax dollars would be to rebuild the village by building better schools and safer communities.

More prisons are not the answer. The love of Christ is the answer. We must get involved with families of those in prison and empower them to break the cycle of misery. Children who have parents in prison are many more times likely to end up in prison themselves. The Church must get involved and claim these children before the legal system does. Our love for Christ must find a practical demonstration in the great needs that surround us. We cannot blindly say that they do not exist or that there is nothing we can do.

What will happen when those in prison are finally released? Where will they get a job? Who will help them rebuild their lives in the village community? Most of the time they discover that they are no better off than when they first went to prison. They lack support of any kind. Because they can't find employment, they have no hope for the future. A return to devastated family structures only make their situations worse. The Church can and must supply a meaningful support for those exiting prison systems and looking for a new start. We can provide a mentoring and training system that will encourage them and help them change the destructive patterns of their lives. Many who are even "saved" in prison return to the streets, and because they have no support system, they unfortunately return to their old life of crime. The shackles that had bound them inside prison are merely replaced by the shackles of a melancholy hopelessness on the outside. It is only the Church that has the anointing to proclaim freedom to these men and women. Remember that but for the grace of God, there go I.

Can You Hear Them Crying?

Can you hear them crying?

We have touched on just a few areas where the sounds of crying can be heard, and to be sure, there are many more. You can hear them if you listen. But there is a crying sound that seems to drown out all others. This other cry is the saddest and unfortunately the loudest of all.

The Loudest Cries of All

The loudest crying is not coming from inside the village, but from inside the Church. For sure, the cries of an immature Church are drowning out all the despondent cries of the lost in the village. We have not been able to raise the village because we have a house full of babies who have refused to grow up and serve the needs that exist in the village around us. We have plugged our ears with devices of immaturity—earplugs of self-centeredness, indifference, and resistance. We cry out for more attention to all our own little bumps and hurts and make idols out of our own pain. We need to be reminded that pain is inevitable; but misery is optional. Jesus never promised us a pain-free life. We can choose to allow our personal pain to become a pathway that releases healing in others.

In John 16:33, Jesus tells us that suffering is a part of the believer's life: "These things I have spoken unto you, that in Me ye might have peace. In the world ye shall have tribulation: but be of good cheer; I have overcome the world." Peter also tells us not to be surprised by the trials and pain that come along: "Beloved, think it not strange concerning the fiery trial which is to try you, as though some strange thing happened unto you" (1 Pet. 4:12).

It is time for the Church to stop crying about her petty wounds and listen to the sounds of crying in the village. If we choose to walk that pathway, we will discover that as we give ourselves to others, our own pain will be healed.

35

It Takes a Church to Raise a Village

After a major stroke in 1993, I was told I would never walk again. The Lord took me to First Samuel 30 and gave me a message called, "Resting Your Tears." In this passage David and his men found that the enemy had invaded Ziklag and had taken their wives and children captive. David and his men wept until they ran out of tears. Then David inquired of the Lord. He was told that if he would pursue his enemies, he would recover all. There was a time that David had to stop grieving and move into action. All the tears in the world were not going to release his family from the hand of the enemy. Until we stop our own crying, we cannot go after others who have been taken prey by the enemy.

We must stop the wail of the immature crying in the Church so that we can give attention to the sound of crying in the village. If we listen closely, we will hear a sobbing sound all around us. But a time is coming when there will no longer be heard in the village the voice of weeping and the sound of crying (see Is. 65:19). It's up to us to hear them crying.

Can you hear them crying?

It Takes a Church to Raise a Village!

Chapter Three

I'm sick and tired of black and white people of good intent giving aspirin to a society that is dying of a cancerous disease.

Ralph Abernathy
U.S. religious and civil rights leader

Chapter Three

No More Manna

And the manna ceased on the morrow after they had eaten of the old corn of the land; neither had the children of Israel manna any more; but they did eat of the fruit of the land of Canaan that year (Joshua 5:12).

A few years ago a young man found his way into our job placement program. We were able to help him find a good job with a local employer. After two weeks, his new employer called our offices looking for him. They said that he had not returned to the job after he received his first paycheck. Somewhat perplexed, we sought him out looking for some kind of explanation to this bizarre behavior. Finally, we found the young man and asked him why he had not returned to his job. He looked at our caseworker with amazement and responded, "They gave me a check. Was I supposed to go back?" It never occurred to him that he would have to continue going back to work to earn more money. Growing up, all he had ever known was that someone regularly sent a check to his family. He thought because he had worked for a few weeks, the employer would continue to mail him a regular paycheck. He did not connect going to work with getting a check because he had simply never seen anyone going to work on a consistent basis.

In another case a lady walked off her new job because she had gotten a call from home saying that her children were arguing. The woman didn't bother to inform a supervisor or talk to anyone in the office. She simply walked out of the office and went home to deal with her children. What seems obvious to us never crossed her mind.

Do these cases sound unbelievable? Maybe so, but they're true. Other similar cases such as these illustrate one of the great realities that confront the Church and particularly the inner-city Church. If we are to raise the village, we must be prepared to deal with the stark reality as it exists in many urban and rural communities: Many families have lived on government assistance for generations and have no concept of a work ethic. The raising of the village must begin with a renewing of the mind, both for those living in the village, as well as the Church. It is interesting to discover that the village has been raised with a welfare mentality that is so similar to that displayed by the children of Israel in the wilderness.

Wandering in the Wilderness

During the time of Israel's wandering in the wilderness, God in His mercy supplied them with food from Heaven. This heavenly provision was called manna. The Bible tells us that "the children of Israel did eat manna forty years, until they came to a land inhabited; they did eat manna, until they came unto the borders of the land of Canaan" (Ex. 16:35). Manna was the food of the wilderness. It was intended to be a temporary solution, not a way of life. Remember, it was not God's intention for Israel to wander through the desert for 40 years, the life span of an entire generation. God's design was that manna would sustain His people until they were prepared for His purpose: possession of the land of Canaan. God said, "Behold, I have set the land before you: go in and possess the land which the Lord sware unto your fathers, Abraham, Isaac, and Jacob, to give unto them and to their seed after them" (Deut. 1:8).

In our time entire generations have been lost as they've wandered in the wilderness sustained by the "manna" of government handouts and church benevolence. Both the Church and the village have lived in bondage to this wilderness mentality that encourages people to depend on others to do for them rather than discovering what they can do for themselves.

Wilderness Mentality of the Village

The manna of the current age is government welfare, which has become a generational curse, preventing those in the village from entering into the best that God has waiting for them.

A life of manna "dries up" the appetite for possession. It diminishes the vitality of life while punishing the hope of those who come to rely upon it. This was exactly what happened to some of the children of Israel who lived on manna in the wilderness. "But now our soul is dried away: there is nothing at all, beside this manna, before our eyes" (Num. 11:6). This Scripture uncovers the real danger of a manna-eating, wilderness-living mentality: The person ceases to exist as he falls away into anonymity. Manna sustains that "wilderness mentality." The village dwellers who subsist in this welfare system are reduced to live lives of paralyzing repetition of meaningless existence that often leads to frustration, anger, and violence. They live as in a fishbowl, trapped behind a glass, as hopeless victims waiting for someone to drop some fish food into their little tank. As long as they remain addicted to this welfare manna, they will never inherit all that God has intended for them.

Another effect of the wilderness thinking is lost opportunity to bless others. My late husband, Dr. Willie Mitchell, Sr., spoke of "the turning of the hand." The palm of the hand is turned upward to receive and downward to impart blessing. Those in the village who live on manna have never had the ability or opportunity to bless others, including their own children. They live in an empty cycle of discontented living, helpless and powerless to break out of its crushing hold. We must empower them by providing help that will turn those hands downward. Hands trained only to benefit from others can be transformed into hands that impart blessing to their next generations.

But first, if we are to alter the wilderness mentality of the village, we must also deal with the wilderness mentality of the Church itself.

Wilderness Mentality of the Church

Unfortunately, the Church has been living in a codependent relationship with the disinherited of the village. In many ways we have sustained the wilderness mentality in the village by focusing our efforts solely on benevolence, handing out more "manna" through our feeding programs. We have made people dependent upon us rather than teaching them to take possession of their destinies.

There is a place for benevolence. Throughout the history of Israel right into the early days of the Church, God's people were responsible to care and provide for those who could not help themselves. We are commanded to care for the fatherless and the widows. James tells us that this is the heart of true religion: "Pure religion and undefiled before God and the Father is this, To visit the fatherless and widows in their affliction, and to keep himself unspotted from the world" (Jas. 1:27). When we provide for the helpless, we are expressing the heart of God who provides grace and mercy to us. "For when we were yet without strength, in due time Christ died for the ungodly" (Rom. 5:6). We must act in kindness and mercy toward those who cannot help themselves. But what of those who are not disabled and are still trapped in this "hands-up" system? We must cease just giving them a handout and begin to give them a hand-up lifting them out of the system.

The distribution of food or sending a check is an easy, religious, feel-good experience. Our codependence manifests itself in our exercise of "good deeds" that gives us a sense of purpose and religious satisfaction. However, good deeds do little to repair the village or empower her people.

We have no sense of spiritual priority as we irresponsibly give money and food to drug abusers who turn around using it to sustain themselves or their families while continuing to abuse drugs. As with all codependent relationships, we enable them to continue destructive lifestyles. For example, the spouse of an abusive mate will allow himself or herself to be abused or make excuses for the abuser, thereby allowing them to continue in their abusiveness. Feeding those caught in the web of drug abuse is like feeding a fly caught in a spider's web. They will still eventually die. We must act now and do something to rescue them from the web of despair and direct them into a new lifestyle. We must cease the business of transference of charity and take up the work of transforming the village.

Benevolence itself is a good thing, but like manna in the wilderness, it is intended to help people in the short term. It is a temporary solution begging for a permanent resolution. We must discover fresh ways to facilitate people's recovery for the long term. We must empower them to possess all that God has intended for them.

Crossing Over to Possession

Before the people in the village can cross over to possess their inheritance, they must be prepared and empowered to do so. It is the responsibility of the Church to prepare the village with job training, supplying job coaches and spiritual mentors. We must provide for practical training in life skills.

There is an old saying that if you give a man a fish, you feed him for a day. But if you teach him to fish, he will feed himself for a lifetime. That is a good and true statement. But why give him just a fishing pole, teaching him an occupation, when we could train him to possess the pond and become the owner/employer?

In Second Kings 4, we read an example of someone who made the transition from poverty to possession. There was a woman, a widowed mother, whose children were being sold into slavery to satisfy a debt. She brought her need to Elisha, the man of God. He asked, "What do you have?" When she responded by telling him that all she had was a single jar of oil, Elisha told her to get the jar and bring it back along with every empty vessel she could lay her hands on. She was told to pour her little bit of oil into the empty vessels. Miraculously, oil continued to pour out of her one tiny jar until all the empty vessels were filled. Then she was told to take the oil, sell some of it to pay the debt, and then *live* off the rest. Note how the Lord responded to her need. He could have merely given her some kind of quick fix or handout to resolve the problem—manna for the moment. But instead, He gave her a means to make money, a way to support her for life. With that business came freedom for her and her children.

The Church must follow the same pattern. First we must ask, "What do you need?" We must recognize the needs that force individuals into the slavery of welfare. Is there a need to raise their level of confidence and hope? Provide spiritual mentors who will help them change their negative mindsets. Is there a need for parenting skills? Offer parenting classes! Is there a need for basic training in life skills? It will do no good to find someone a job and then have them lose it because they can't get up in time to go to work. Buy them an alarm clock!

Then we must ask, "What do you have in the house?" (See Second Kings 4:2.) We must find out what kind of abilities they have and multiply those skills through job training. But it is not enough to give them knowledge or a skill; we must also provide job coaches and mentors to walk alongside them. Who are the retired of your congregation? Perhaps they can become the true elders and mentors in the village.

The key to transforming the mind-set of the Church is to teach them to take personal responsibility for the village one family at a time.

The key to transforming the mind-set of the Church is to teach them to take personal responsibility for the village one family at a time. "God setteth the solitary in families: He bringeth out those which are bound with chains: but the rebellious dwell in a dry land" (Ps. 68:6). We must accept personal responsibility that reaches beyond government social programs and anemic church schemes. We must bring the lost of the village into our families. The government has proven that money alone will never solve the problems of the village or fulfill their needs. Through personal relationships we can transform those enslaved in the village.

There might even be some "lost in the welfare/wilderness mentality" sitting in the pews of your congregation. Our congregation has been able to help every family in our church get off welfare and find meaningful jobs or even develop their own businesses. One lady from our congregation who was on welfare was placed in a job-training program and became a welder. She now owns her own welding business and is a subcontractor to larger construction companies. She went from welfare to welding because of the Church's active involvement in her life. The government gave her a fish. The Church gave her a life, by equipping her to buy a piece of the pond.

Another woman sent us a letter about her experience with the Church. Part of that letter follows:

"On July 5, 2000 I went to the local Human Services Department and asked for help—not a welfare—but for training so I could get out and become a responsible member of society once again. This was where my experience began.

"My case work manager had the foresight to place me in an innovative program called Family W.O.R.K.S., which is part of Project Impact-Dayton, Inc. This program did have an impact on my life. They showed me how to believe in myself and the things that I could do to help myself. They gave me skills to pursue a career and taught me to use the skills I have acquired from other life experiences. They genuinely cared about each person in the class I was part of. I would recommend this program to anyone who wants to put their lives back together...Every day I thank God for bringing me to this wonderful group...they had faith and believed in me."

Preparing for the Harvest of Promise

Get ready for the greatest Church growth program in history: welfare reform. The government has spent money and created programs, yet they have had little effect on the village and can no longer manage its growing needs.

Welfare reform will create the opportunity to transform the lives of those in the village. Once the village finds out that the government is out of money, their desperation will lead them to your door because the first place desperate people go is the church. Whether you have a storefront or a steeple, the needy of the village will find you. And when they do, you must be prepared for them.

When the village comes to your door, preaching at them will not be enough. You will no longer be able to have church as usual. When the village comes to your door, you must move beyond simply being satisfied to exercise your gifts within the walls of the church. Those gifts and abilities that Christ gave us were for the benefit of the village—to win them to Christ; to help them cross over to promise; to give them hope; to give them a life! The present-day Church wants to experience the power of the first-century Church, but they have not taken up the responsibility for that which the power was given. We have done *church work*, but now we must do *the work of the Church*.

The time has come to wean the village from wilderness food and teach them to produce food by their own hands made in the land of promise. As we turn our eyes and our hearts towards the village, we will see the manifestation of the true anointing and power of God released as never before.

There is no more manna.

It Takes a Church to Raise a Village!

Chapter Four

The key to understanding our part is the realization that God only moves forward with his redemptive plan through people who are prepared to receive freely and cooperate with him in the next step.

Dallas Willard
American author

Chapter Four

From Empires to Empowerment

Now Peter and John went up together into the temple at the hour of prayer, being the ninth hour. And a certain man lame from his mother's womb was carried, whom they laid daily at the gate of the temple which is called Beautiful, to ask alms of them that entered into the temple; who seeing Peter and John about to go into the temple asked an alms. And Peter, fastening his eyes upon him with John, said, Look on us. And he gave heed unto them, expecting to receive something of them. Then Peter said, Silver and gold have I none; but such as I have give I thee: In the name of Jesus Christ of Nazareth rise up and walk (Acts 3:1-6).

Up until this point, we have discussed what the Church needs to *see*—the desperate needs of the village that surrounds it. Now we must further engage the critical issue of what the Church should *think*—changing our mind-set from one of wilderness to possession. This new mind-set will of necessity include what we must *build*. What is the Church of Jesus Christ building? We have a crucial choice to make. Will we choose to focus on building our own impressive *empires* of religion, or will we turn our attention to building a new village, *empowering* those who sit at our very gates?

Acts 3:1-6 symbolically presents a compelling illustration that will guide us in this new building program for the village. It is the account of a man who was daily "carried" to the temple gate. Religion offered him no other alternative but a beggar's lifestyle. He was an exile prohibited from the benefits of participation in the community of God's people. As a castaway, he was placed at the gate of the temple reduced to living off the alms of those religious folks who passed by. This was the gate "Beautiful," a very ornate and impressive doorway into the temple that was covered with gold and other precious metals. Throughout his years of begging, thousands of people had passed him by, oblivious to his desperate need. Their good deeds and noble intentions had only served to sustain his beggarly existence. They had helped him live another day, and yet he remained *unhealed*. His miserable life provided an opportunity for devout Jews to display their generosity by righteous acts of charitable giving as they quickly entered the temple to get on with the serious business of religious exercises. He was the object of the righteous pity of a religious system, but remained *unhealed*.

Then one day Peter and John passed by at the hour of sacrifice, the time when religious men perform their duty. As Peter was about to enter the temple, his heart was seized by this man's condition. He turned towards him with a fixed gaze that spoke a million words. Peter, on his way to church, shifted his attention away from the opulent beauty of the religious structure and locked his eyes on this lame man. No one had ever looked at him in this way. The gaze was not a look of pity, but was full of compassion and desire. Peter then spoke out of the deep compassion of his heart and in essence said, "I don't have any worldly thing to impress you with, but I do have something that will change your life and put you on your feet. Rise up in Jesus Christ!" Peter made a decision that day. He chose to set aside religious duty and righteous appearance so that he could change one man's life forever. He did not look upon this poverty-stricken man as an outsider, but welcomed him into the community and that day gave him a purpose and inheritance.

There are so very many who sit at our gates: socially and spiritually lame from the womb, socially disenfranchised, generationally dysfunctional, educationally disadvantaged, and personally impoverished. What will we do? How will we respond to those who sit at our gates? Will we continue to pass them by as we make our way to our own houses of worship?

Or will we open our eyes and take notice of them? Will we reach out and take them by the hand as Peter did, raising them up in the name of Jesus Christ? Will we seek to *impress* the village temporarily with our pious endeavors, or will we *impact* their lives eternally with our compassionate exploits?

Impressing or Impacting

Once I was privileged to visit Buckingham Palace, official town residence of the British monarch since 1837, located near Saint James's Park, London. John Nash remodeled this neoclassical structure in 1825. In 1856 a ballroom was added, and in 1913 a new east front was built. Buckingham Palace has about 600 rooms and 20 hectares (50 acres) of gardens. It is noted for its fine collection of paintings.

I especially loved the Changing of the Guard at its main gate. With an hourly precision performance of this ceremony, the soldiers march in lock step, outwardly oblivious to the surrounding environment. They are intent on one thing, the formal procedure at hand. The ritual is dignified and thrilling to watch.

Suddenly I was struck by another reality soberly hanging over this majestic sight. I solemnly considered the facts as they drifted into my thoughts. The residents of the palace, the royal monarchy, have only a symbolic semblance of power. The real power now resides in the parliament of England. For the most part, those of the royal family socially remain inside their protective walls untouched by the condition of those who live around them and are powerless to make changes. Enormous amounts of money are spent to maintain their royal lifestyle, maintaining an artificial sense of authority and regal power. They may be *impressive* in all their regal appearance, but they have little *impact* on their subjects.

We in the Church have similarly set about trying to *impress* each other with our own stately form and prosperity. We despise those who are financially deprived in the ministry and look down on them as though they have missed God. Worldly wealth has become the new measure of spiritual status. We seek to impress one another in the Body with our big cars and expensive clothes. We have become so prosperity conscious that we have developed our own prosperity doctrine.

We have sought to *impress* one another with our bigger and grander facilities costing millions of dollars. We take pride in the number of people who are attracted to our glorious structures. (These are usually those who left other less impressive facilities.) There is a spirit of competition among churches as we build impressive monuments, testimonies to our own material motivations.

We seek to *impress* the world by creating our own spiritual royalty in the form of "superstar preachers" who hold us spellbound with mysterious revelation and oratorical skill. Unfortunately, we walk out of those meetings quickly forgetting those impressive words that have no relevance to our daily existence. The sermons that are preached should direct our attention to the need of the village rather than feeding us words that only make us spiritually fat and complacent to those on the outside of our own walls.

We also try to *impress* one another with the good works that we religiously perform. We feel good at Christmastime handing out turkeys to the poor in the village, and some of us even go as far as giving away some old clothing or used furniture that we have replaced with something much finer. I don't want to minimize the need to help in these material ways, but if we never go beyond these minimal efforts, we are only temporarily resolving their problems.

Preachers spend many hours per week preparing sermons to *impress* and dazzle their congregations while little is done in the way of equipping saints to establish their own ministries. In fact, ministry seems to be the role of only a very few. We burn out a small staff of pastors who can never effectively meet all the needs of the congregation let alone those in the village. We are facing the need for a major paradigm shift in how the Body of Christ functions.

In our own ministry, we have experienced this shifting of focus. When we first began our ministry in Dayton, I regularly walked past a large, mainline denominational church building. It was very beautiful, but not very functional. Its occupants met there two or three hours per week. I had actually inquired at one point whether they might be willing to sell the facility to us. I was told in derision that they would never consider selling the building—a meaningless monument in the community.

The Lord began to lay a burden on my heart to redeem this facility for the Kingdom of God. I would stop and touch the bricks of the building, speaking to them and claiming them for the Kingdom. I am sure that those who observed this strange behavior thought I was in need of some kind of therapy. But as I continued to pray in faith for this building, the Lord lit a fire in some of the people of that congregation. They began to get a burden to move beyond *having church* to start *being the Church*. This eventually resulted in many leaving the congregation so that those who remained were unable to financially support the facilities. They were eventually forced to sell the building for far less than they originally paid to build it. We were able to purchase that building with finances provided by God,

It's time to shift the momentum from building our own kingdoms to repairing the village.

and we did redeem it for His Kingdom. It ultimately became a hub of spiritual ministry to the village, constantly being used for a variety of community services.

59

We have invested in impressive preachers. We have invested in impressive facilities. We have invested in impressive numerical growth (mostly by transferring believers). But we have failed to invest in the village. It's time to shift the momentum from building our own kingdoms to repairing the village. It's time to establish new priorities!

Setting Kingdom Priorities

If the Church is to move beyond hollow attempts at impressing the village with temporary solutions to generational problems, then we have to shift our vision of constructing religious empires strategically positioned to block village dwellers from entering. If we are to impact the village, we have to establish new priorities for our time and the Lord's money—new priorities that concentrate on the building up of the Church, the people of God, rather than focus on supporting the buildings of the church. Our priority must become the establishment of the Kingdom of God in the midst of the village.

Our first concern must begin with focusing resources toward the village. When we build new facilities, they need to accommodate ministry towards the village. Are we building multipurpose facilities that invite ministry? Are we building classrooms for education or Taj Mahal-type facilities for religious display? Before we spend the Lord's money, we should be clear on whose purpose we are serving: the Lord's or our own. Whose glory are we manifesting? The Church should exist for the glory of God, not our own. "Unto Him be glory in the church by Christ Jesus throughout all ages, world without end. Amen" (Eph. 3:21). Our facilities should support the ministry of the Church rather than the Church having to support empty, irrelevant facilities. It seems that we can always raise money to build new buildings, but then struggle to find funds to meet the pressing needs of the village.

From Empires to Empowerment

Another Kingdom priority is shifting the spotlight of ministry from the few to the whole Body. We must equip and empower the whole *Body* in the ministry of the *Head*. If we are to restore the village, it will take a corporate effort—a team rather than an individual, a symphony rather than a solo.

A third spiritual shift involves changing our church programs, especially our youth programs in the village. As we stated earlier, the youth programs of our churches can become valuable tools to reach the lost youth in the village. Rather than merely entertaining the youth of the congregations, we can teach them to reach out to the village. When we have church social functions, we should invite others in the neighborhood to join us at the table. We should plan meaningful events that can be a significant experience for those inside and outside our walls as well.

All our efforts should not be centered on attracting people to come to us. Rather, we must get involved in the life of the village. We cannot restrict the Body of Christ to minister solely inside the church walls. We must become an occupying army of the Kingdom of God and move forward from house to house in the village. Where does the Kingdom reign of God end? Does it not go beyond the walls of the righteous? Is there some imaginary line that God cannot cross? Is God not concerned with the life of the village?

All areas of life are God's business, and we should pay attention and get involved. Why should we not run for public office? Why should we not get involved with other secular efforts to rebuild the village? If God is concerned, we should be also.

We must shift the emphasis from church order and government to the believer's effective involvement in the world all around him. We spend valuable time in the pulpit talking about ourselves, our government, our order, our ambition, rather than creating strategies that will transform the village. Jesus was not that concerned about church government. He was concerned with reaching those on the outer fringes of society and lifting them out of their misery. Jesus insisted that His disciples not govern as the Gentiles, but instructed them to fashion their lives as a servant (see Mk. 10:42-43). Jesus was not concerned with ruling over man; He was concerned with relating to man.

Empowerment

God has given us effective resources that will empower the village, enabling them to rebuild for themselves. The most compelling tools we have are our own people. I like to call them the "jewels in the pews." Few pastors are aware of this incredible resource. They are so concerned about fulfilling their own vision that they have lost sight of the abilities and influence of those in the church. There is more potential power in the pew than behind the pulpit. Are they teachers? Are they plumbers? What kinds of certifications do they hold? What kind of training might they have? Go on a treasure hunt and you'll discover the valuable wealth and precious jewels who have been sitting in the pew, waiting to be found.

We must become modern "Nehemiahs" and carefully survey the damage to the village walls. As we prayerfully consider the condition of the village, God will give us carefully constructed plans for rebuilding the waste places. We will discover the proper people to strategically position in critical places for village reconstruction. If the people of the congregation sense the clear calling and power of God, they will give of themselves to do the work. "Thy people shall be willing in the day of thy power" (Ps. 110:3a).

We must understand that every village has distinct and different needs that are unique to their circumstances. For some, there will be serious problems with drugs. Others might have an unusual number of single mothers who need help with parenting skills and job training. Some communities will need to develop literacy programs for those with learning difficulties. Other communities will need to look into developing centers for ministering to those with AIDS. Make a careful analysis of your community. Prepare a survey that will identify the skills in your community. Who in your congregation can teach others to read? Maybe there are retired schoolteachers who can be used in literacy programs? Are there those who can do crisis counseling? How about those who would be willing to visit prisoners and develop programs for them when they are released? If you give your heart to it, the Lord will quickly begin to give you insight and strategies for the particular needs in your community.

Do not be overwhelmed by the needs around you. Choose one area and begin there. Don't try to do too much. Be sensitive to the Spirit's direction. Be patient as you build bridges into the village. Let your faith rise up and embrace the challenges before you.

And the King shall answer and say unto them, Verily I say unto you, Inasmuch as ye have done it unto one of the least of these My brethren, ye have done it unto Me (Matthew 25:40).

We must also not fail to take into account the life experiences of those in our congregations. Those who have been wounded can become wounded healers to others in the village. My husband had spent most of his ministry reaching out to the young men of the village. One young man was a notorious drug dealer. Through many trials and with much patience, my husband led him to the Lord, and he became a respectable member of the community. Who better to counsel others in bondage to drugs? Religion might see a person's past history and problems as proof of unfitness, but those very problems can become qualification for ministry to others who still struggle. They may comfort with the same "comfort wherewith we ourselves are comforted of God" (2 Cor. 1:4b). You have more tools than you know. Find out who they are and place them in ministry to the village.

Churches can be transformed to empowerment centers. Our church has established what is called "Project Impact," which can be set up in your local church as well. Our mission is to equip families and children for success. Our goal is to become the agency of choice for stabilizing and strengthening families. Our desire is to see strong, healthy, and self-sufficient families in committed relationships, contributing to the well-being of their communities. All families, regardless of economic and social backgrounds, have the ability to succeed if we equip them with the knowledge and skills to do so. (See Appendix C for a full schematic of Project Impact.)

God is calling us out of the temple and into the village. It will require that we refocus our attention. We must move from impressing the village with our stately structures to impacting it with the power of God through the tools that He has provided. The future of the village is in our hands.

It Takes a Church to Raise a Village!

Chapter Five

True social progress can never be effected solely by programmes of reform, organised demand, and legislative action. High wages and abundant leisure, good housing and improved sanitation, are not able of themselves to guarantee progress or even to check deterioration. It is of far greater importance that people should be clean and sober in their habits, and thrifty in their use of time and money, and that all the relationships of the members of a community should be inspired by love rather than controlled by principles of legal justice and economic equality: and these things are most surely promoted by the presence of earnest Christians living ascetically in the midst of society under various types of organization.

O. Hardman
American author

Chapter
Five

Daddy's Truck and a King's Command

But ye shall receive power, after that the Holy Ghost is come upon you: and ye shall be witnesses unto Me both in Jerusalem, and in all Judaea, and in Samaria, and unto the uttermost part of the earth (Acts 1:8).

Daddy was the owner and operator of a local refuse hauling company in Pittsburgh, Pennsylvania. His main business was hauling scrap metal in his old truck. But that truck carried much more than scrap metal. It carried the presence of Jesus Christ throughout our north-side neighborhood.

On many occasions my dad, Elder Davis, or "Brother Jack," as he was affectionately called, would clean out his scrap metal truck and transform it into a transporter of wonderful treasures into the local neighborhood. He loaded his truck with everything from clothing to food to toys and anything else he could find for a bargain. He would often visit the local produce distributor and purchase all kinds of vegetables or canned goods that would then be delivered to those in need.

I fondly recall one Easter when Dad was given hundreds of pink, yellow, and blue chicks and ducklings from a pet store owner who was unable to sell all of them. Many temporary chicken coops were built all over the neighborhood as Dad delivered these multicolored peeps. The children were so thrilled to have these "pets," even if for just a short while, before their parents would prepare them for the dinner table.

Dad would often allow us kids to make these precious deliveries. We were always greeted with such joy and excitement. I believe those experiences were the seeds that were planted and watered and eventually led to a vision to raise the village. I'm sure that my parents never realized the importance of that great work. They were just merely passing on blessings from God. My parents did not think in terms of raising a village, but they did raise me along with two boys who were not their own by blood. I believe we were blessed with abundance because my dad understood the principle of sowing and reaping, and he freely gave because he was given so much.

Along with food, my dad's truck also carried hope to the people who were unemployed. He would create jobs for them by allowing them to help out in his business. Sometimes he would even bring these men home at the end of the day.

Once I remember Dad introducing us to a dark-skinned, older man with snow-white hair and a deeply furrowed brow. After we had served him dinner complete with a luscious dessert, my dad drove him to a local bathhouse to clean up. Upon their return, we discovered, to our amazement, that the man's skin was as white as his hair. Our mission in this man's life had only begun. He sat at our table many times as Dad shared with him the spiritual food of the gospel. As it turned out, he was one of many who would eventually receive blessing from the Lord's table in our home. Our six-room row home on the north side of Pittsburgh was a haven of hope for many.

My dad was also the pastor of a small congregation. He began his ministry on Sunday mornings by feeding the hungry before Sunday school. When the hunger had been satisfied in their bellies, they were then able to receive spiritual food for their souls from the Word of God. Many people merely came to see what kind of person would so freely give of himself and his material blessings. Many left the services with their lives changed forever. In our congregation there was no one with a need that was not met by my dad's generous care. No child was abandoned, and no one ever went hungry.

Yes, Dad's truck was used for more than just hauling scrap metal or food for the hungry. He carried with him the living witness of Jesus Christ. He knew a lot about raising a village long before Hillary Clinton's book. He impacted our village one truckload at a time.

At my mother's "homegoing"service in 1999, my dad was overwhelmed by the love that poured out to him from many generations who had been touched by the kindness of Jesus Christ through my parents. During the 63 years of my parents' marriage, numerous people found hope and healing under their roof. For John and Ruby Davis, raising a village began right there at our home.

Jesus declared that we are to be His witnesses. A witness is one who corroborates the truth. Jesus told His disciples that they would be witnesses in Jerusalem, Judea, Samaria, and then to the uttermost parts of the world. More than that, Jesus was going to empower them to be witnesses. This spiritual power was not only to be used inside the walls of a church; but it was also given for the purpose of bearing witness to His resurrection and declaring the hope of the gospel to the lost living outside those walls.

It is unfortunate how we have misused His power and misrepresented His purpose. We gather together on Sunday mornings in our holy sanctuaries in an effort to impress one another with those precious gifts—gifts that Jesus meant to be used in redeeming a broken world. We are to give evidence of the love and mercy of Jesus Christ to the world, but instead we have kept the testimony hidden behind our beloved church walls.

Jesus gave us the "great commission"; but as part of our lives, it is often found to be the "small omission." He said, "Go ye therefore, and teach all nations, baptizing them in the name of the Father, and of the Son, and of the Holy Ghost: teaching them to observe all things whatsoever I have commanded you: and, lo, I am with you always, even unto the end of the world" (Mt. 28:19-20). This is no idle suggestion. It is a command from our supreme Commander charging us to go! It is not an option; it is an obligation.

Accompanying this command from Jesus is a pattern to follow. He told us to begin in Jerusalem, then go to Judea, Samaria, and the ends of the earth. We have reversed the order. We think of missions in terms of the mystique, going to far-away countries and helping children with bloated bellies. What if those TV cameras that document the plight of those living in distant lands would be turned on the streets of our own villages? What would they see? Would those cases make us weep, as do the pictures from Africa, Bosnia, or India? Don't misunderstand me; I am not suggesting that the Church abandon her mission in other parts of the world. There is still so much we can do. But we must also think in terms of our local missions to the villages of our own precious country.

In 1999 I was on a trip to Nairobi, Kenya, where we had built a children's home. As I watched the children of that village playing in the streets, God spoke to my heart about the children in our own villages. These children are no less in need than those in Africa, yet we spend so much more money and emotion on the children in foreign lands than we do for the children, living down the street outside the security gates of our churches, who remain hungry and hopeless. We must not ignore those in our own backyard. The Bible says, "But if anyone does not provide for his own, and especially for those of his household, he has denied the faith and is worse than an unbeliever" (1 Tim. 5:8 NAS).

Daddy Truck and a King's Command

When I returned home, this vision for our own village overshadowed my every thought. I began to immediately pursue the vision by investing in the lives of the children of our own village. I now have a new understanding and appreciation for the pattern that Jesus laid out for His followers. I believe this plan of our Lord begins right in our own neighborhoods. Our backyard is our Jerusalem. Judea can be compared to our cities and Samaria to those who are her outcasts. When we have been faithful to care for our own, then we can effectively go to the outermost parts of the world. But we must begin right on our own streets.

We have become comfortable and careless within the walls of our congregations. We need to reach out as my dad did, clearing out the refuse of self-centered thinking and begin carrying the hope and life of Jesus Christ to the village. Three words to direct us in the unfolding of the great commission of Jesus Christ are *command, compassion,* and *commitment.*

First, Jesus gave a *command.* As Americans, we are not too good at taking orders. We are used to deciding everything by consensus. But the Kingdom of God is not a democracy where everyone does as he chooses. Jesus prayed, "Thy Kingdom come, Thy will be done." The Kingdom comes when His will is done. Our part is to discover His will and live our lives in complete submission to that manifested will. Our lives are no longer our own; they belong to Jesus. We are crucified and now live by faith in the Son of God (see Gal. 2:20). When He says, "Go," we pack our bags and go! We must make the raising of the village our priority, not our pastime.

Compassion is an action that is best demonstrated rather than discussed. True compassion is substantiated in a love flowing out of our hearts to meet a troubled soul. "But whoso hath this world's good, and seeth his brother have need, and shutteth up his bowels of compassion from him, how dwelleth the love of God in him?" (1 Jn. 3:17) It was in compassion that the Father sent the Son of His love. That divine love reached out of Heaven and healed our broken lives. This compassion was felt by One who had the power to reverse the curse of human sickness and societal devolution. Jesus reached out and "touched" the unclean and the rejected, lifting them to a place of wholeness. That same compassion and power has been transferred to us. We are to carry out the mission that was started by our Lord. If we see a brother or sister who is homeless or hopeless, and ignore their condition, how can we pretend to have the love of God? How can we not be willing to reach out and "touch" them, lifting them out of their desperate situation?

Once my mother was on an evangelistic outreach and was given gospel tracts to hand out to the lost. As she went out on this gospel mission, she eventually came across a group of hungry and cold people. Standing there in front of them she refused to distribute the tracts. She was convinced that it would be cruel to hand a hungry man a piece of paper without first meeting his needs. It is so easy to hand out a tract and walk away thinking we have fulfilled our religious obligation to the lost. However, true love demands that we get involved and that we care for the whole man, not just his soul. We must stop pretending we are the Church and start performing acts of mercy on those around us. Let's exchange our gospel tracts for compassionate acts.

We must release the dynamic power of Jesus on the village. Let's release *apostles* to establish agencies that will rebuild the village. We can send out *prophets* who will give us prophetic direction and empower us with a renewed burden for the village. We must loose *pastors* in our pews who can provide loving care for those whose lives are burdened with the tragedies of life. We must all become *evangelists* living the good news and introducing people to the living reality of our Christ. We must walk through our doors out into the streets empowered with the *compassion* of our Lord.

We must enter into the village and lift her residents out of their destitution and despair. We have the capability of equipping them to rebuild their families. We have the resources to provide. We can step into the middle of their hopeless existence, take them by the hand, and lead them into a place that will give them a life that has meaning and purpose.

His strategy was to empower the company of the disenfranchised and bring down the oppressive conditions that surround the people of His love.

The depth of Jesus' love for the poor and needy originated from the throne. We should not be surprised by His deep compassion for those who dwell on the outer fringes of human existence. Jesus came in the spirit of His Father—the spirit of love for the lost, care for the poor, and wholeness for the broken. His strategy was to empower the company of the disenfranchised and bring down the oppressive conditions that surround the people of His love. He transferred the love in His heart to His disciples and sent them forth to deliver that love and liberty to all. "But when He saw the multitudes, He was moved with compassion on them, because they fainted, and were scattered abroad, as sheep having no shepherd. Then saith He unto His disciples, The harvest truly is plenteous, but the labourers are few; pray ye therefore the Lord of the harvest, that He will send forth labourers into His harvest" (Mt. 9:36-38). You and I are the workers. We are the answer to Jesus' prayer for more laborers, and our harvest is the village.

The Body of Christ must be *committed* to raise the village. To be committed means to recognize the seriousness of the mission and then dedicate all that we have to the work of rebuilding, despite the cost. Jesus did not consider the cost when it came to His own personal mission. He was prepared to take His mission to its finality on the cross. His disciples were prepared to take that mission into the world, and now it is our turn to continue that mission in our own world.

We struggle today with the word *commitment* whether it's in a marriage or a ministry. No one wants to take the time or pay the price to get involved in change. Raising the village must become a lifestyle as surely as it was for my dad. I believe that he carried trash only during the day so that he could carry the love of Jesus to the village in the evening. Love was a habit with him. It was a lifestyle. He was committed to Jesus Christ and His eternal purposes.

There are no more excuses! We say that we have no time, no money, and no volunteers to do the work. If that is the case, then we must set new priorities for our churches. We must consecrate ourselves to the full preaching of the whole truth of the gospel. That truth is not for us alone but to be shared with the village. Unfortunately, we have become too involved with our own lives, working two or three jobs to get ahead. Our children are involved in every sport and activity while being deprived of the joy of ministry to others. We say we will win the lost, but only depending on the cost. How much is a soul worth to you? Where God gives us vision, there is always provision. We must give everything to raise the village. We must get out of the pews and into the streets and go get those who are lost!

I recall a time when a mother in our congregation had a son who was lost in the horrid world of drugs. She could have given in to her grief and disappeared in hopeless despair. But she decided to take back what the devil had stolen from her. She was going to find her son and bring him back. She and

Daddy Truck and a King's Command

some others in the church made up posters bearing the picture of her son that read "Wanted by Jesus Christ, family and friends." They distributed the flyers throughout the neighborhoods where drugs were rampant. On one occasion she ran into a young boy who expressed his wish that someone love him as much as she had demonstrated in launching this campaign.

Finally, she came across a lady who saw the flyer and said that she knew where her son was living. She led her to the apartment building where she had seen him. The mother went to the door of the apartment and knocked. A girl met her at the door and then violently slammed it in her face. But she refused to give up. She stapled flyers to the door of the apartment and prayed with her friends. She went to the door one more time and knocked. This time, her son came rushing through the door, weeping in repentance. She had her son back. They put him in the van and took him home.

That Sunday another boy with the same problem showed up in church and gave his life to Jesus. If only we would get involved, we could change the atmosphere in the village. We need to speak out, and with acts of compassion, demonstrate our love for the sons and daughters of the village. We need to let them know that Jesus has sent a rescue party specifically for their deliverance. It can only happen when we respond to the *command* with *compassion* and *commitment.*

In closing, let me declare with all the passion in my heart that we must begin now to do the work of rebuilding and raising the village. Jesus has given us the power and the plan for that rebuilding process. We must start this very moment to use that power in our own Jerusalem.

I long to see a new age of the Church dawning. It will be a new Church that is moved with compassion to change the village. The time is right. The mission is ours. Let the process begin. *It Takes a Church to Raise a Village!*

Chapter Six

The great end of life is not knowledge but action.
Thomas Henry Huxley
English biologist

Chapter
Six

Association of the Church and State

But Jehoshaphat said, Is there not here a prophet of the Lord, that we may inquire of the Lord by him? And one of the king of Israel's servants answered and said, Here is Elisha the son of Shaphat, which poured water on the hands of Elijah (2 Kings 3:11).

The Bible contains many occurrences when a king of Israel, threatened by calamitous circumstances, sought divine wisdom from God through the prophets. On one such occasion, Jehoshaphat, the king of Judah, and Jehoram, king of Israel, moved in unison to confront the rebellion of the king of Moab. Wandering around in the wilderness and desperate for water and direction, King Jehoshaphat cried out, "Is there not a prophet of the Lord here?" One of the king's servants directed Jehoshaphat to the prophet Elisha who in turn brought prophetic direction to a political dispute.

Most people in both the religious as well as the secular community have believed the lie of the politically correct philosophy of "separation of church and state." Each side has rigorously avoided being affected by the other. As the lines of separation between the two intensify, the urban village, an unfortunate victim, continues in darkness. Unfortunately, neither the church[1] nor the state understand the power of a cooperative endeavor that could eventually bring hope and healing to the village. Instead of a "separation of church and state," we need to begin thinking in terms of an "association of the church and state." Both the church and the government need

83

to apply themselves to the tearing down of the dividing wall that has alienated them from each other. They must discover a way to overcome the fear of being controlled by one another. Together a formidable force could be formed to rebuild our defiled and disintegrating village.

Is there a legal and moral relationship between church and state? How can we partner with one another? Can we discover a base that will allow us to work together for a common cause?

In order to understand more accurately what the founding fathers intended, let us look at the Constitution of the United States.

A Separation of the Mind

Article I of the United States Constitution reads, "*Congress shall make no law respecting an establishment of religion, or prohibiting the free exercise thereof....*" This one line has been falsely interpreted by liberals to mean a *separation* between church and state. They have used the phrase "*shall make no law...*" as a means of promoting their own agenda, thus excluding the moral values of Christianity as a standard for any kind of civic action. The phrase "separation of church and state" has been overused to the point that most people believe it comes directly from the Constitution. However, this part of the Constitution refers to government establishing its own official denomination like the Church of England. The framers of the Constitution were seeking to avoid a state religion that would in some way limit the free exercise of religion according to each man's conscience. The Constitution was never meant to protect us *from* religion; it affirms the free exercise of religion protecting its participants from government control. The fact is there can never be a strict separation of church and state. It is simply an illusion in the liberal mind.

Association of the Church and State

Gradually over the years, the government has built higher and more defined walls that have hindered the free exercise of religion. One of the most devastating effects of this hideous philosophy is the influence it has had in our schools. Laws have been passed making it "illegal" to pray in public schools. I can hear the sound of our founding fathers rolling over in their graves. This must be an abuse of the Constitution beyond their wildest imagination.

Nevertheless, we are deluded if we think we can actually take prayer out of the school. Prayer can never be taken out of schools, because it is a spiritual matter between believers and their Lord. The government has no power to interrupt an intimate conversation between a student and God. We may not pray over the loudspeaker or lead in prayer in the classroom, but prayer can never be removed from the schools.

There is a unique bond between our Judaic/Christian heritage and the foundations of our government. They are woven together like a fine cloth that cannot be separated without destroying the whole. From the very formative days of this country, God's handprint has covered every aspect of our "civil" lives. We are surrounded by those religious influences from the inscription on the Liberty Bell in Philadelphia taken from Leviticus 25:10: *"Proclaim liberty throughout the land to all the inhabitants thereof,"* to our currency which reads, "In God we trust." Each day Congress begins with a chaplain praying in the chambers of government beseeching God's divine favor on our elected leaders. The very fabric of our civil law codes are spun from the spool of the Ten Commandments, although now those same Ten Commandments are no longer allowed to be posted in our schools and public buildings. With the gradual decline of Christianity's influence in our government, there is a certain angst that hangs over our country.

The principles of the Ten Commandments are a reflection of the righteousness of God and find some evidence in every person created in God's image. "For the invisible things of Him from the creation of the world are clearly seen, being understood by the things that are made, even His eternal power and Godhead; so that they are without excuse" (Rom. 1:20). So, it is impossible to exempt the truths of the Ten Commandments or prayer out of schools and courthouses. They will always manifest themselves in the lives of those who have been transformed by the power of Christ.

Many educated people from schools such as Harvard and Yale are involved in the ongoing building of the walls of separation from religion. Ironically, these colleges and universities where they received their degrees and credentials were established upon Christian foundations. "Professing themselves to be wise, they became fools" (Rom. 1:22). They deny the very presence of God in the institutions that were built to represent Him.

We could go on listing one influence after another where Christianity has impacted the founding and the formation of our beloved country. Our major argument is, there is no real separation between the church and the society. *We have believed a lie.*

Now it is our task to get out a spiritual sledgehammer and begin demolishing the walls that divide our faith and our community. We must destroy every force that seeks to contain us. It is quite clear that the government by itself has run out of answers. However, desperate people will find a way to climb over or tunnel under those walls just as they did at the wall that divided Germany. They found their way to hope and freedom.

It does seem as though the government is becoming increasingly aware of the power of the church to create societal reform at all levels. Shortly after the resolution of the 2000 presidential election, on a TV network news program I heard former Speaker of the House Newt Gingrich speak favorably regarding President Bush's proposed cooperation with faith-based institutions. He also mentioned the success of certain Prison Fellowship programs in reducing the rate of recidivism—repeat crime and incarnation—at selected prisons. I am encouraged to believe that real possibilities exist for government and church to work together in a positive way.

Tearing Down the Walls of Separation

Around Our Schools

Although school officials will not allow us to preach sermons or lead prayer on their premises, they cannot stop us from scheduling prayer walks around the school grounds after hours. We urge each congregation to adopt a local school and to pray for that school, including its principal, teachers, and students. We have been too willing to abandon our public schools. We must rise up and take them back in the name of the Lord.

Many schools have expressed their gratitude for our church's prayers and have reported positive changes in the classrooms. One local school called me to administrate a cooperative effort between the neighborhood schools and the local churches. I think we are too quick to judge our schools. We might be surprised how willing they are to have our involvement. It is not enough for Christians to meet one day a year at the flagpole to pray. This is a great start, but we need a more creative and consistent effort to bring change to our schools.

The schools want to elicit our support in providing practical solutions. But the church is so often more occupied in addressing the problems than with getting involved in creating the solutions. Church leaders should organize meetings with local school authorities for the purpose of discussing the issues confronting their schools. Together maybe they can find constructive remedies for alarming conditions. We must take responsibility to help schools beyond insisting on Bible studies and prayer meetings. The church can work hand in hand with our schools putting forth compassionate responses rather than presiding over memorial services for tragic victims.

The government has legislated against God and Christian values in our schools. This unfortunate legislation has led to a breakdown of the family. Schools are now reaping the lack of Christian influence, as we watch the disastrous parade of increased violence toward students and teachers alike. The church can step into that pitiful void created by the absence of biblical standards and positive role models. They can provide ethical materials and a positive demonstration of those values. There is a rising realization that we need those very biblical values brought back into the schools if they are to ever recover. We are watching a new emphasis being placed on character development based in biblical values.

Our program "Project Impact" has developed a good relationship with our local schools. This relationship with the schools is so positive that they actually call us to deal with students who get into trouble for fighting or who have other social problems. In one particular incident, a student had attacked a teacher. One teacher quickly responded asking the school to call the police. From another direction someone cried out, "Call Project Impact." Both were called and arrived at the same time. We were able to have the children released to us rather than having them taken into police custody. The police have the authority to haul a student off and place him in incarceration; Project Impact has the power to love them back into the classroom.

We also are actively involved in dealing with the constant problem of truancy. We initiated a new program called

"S.T.A.N.D." (Students Taking A New Direction) that helps students deal with social and academic problems. Each school has its own unique needs. If you are really concerned enough about your school, find out what the problems are and how you can be a part of the solution. It is easy to complain and criticize. It takes more effort to set aside a judgmental spirit and get involved in the answer.

The schools of the village are crying out for our help. I recommend that pastors visit their schools at the beginning of the school year. Make your presence known to them and let them know you are available to assist in any way.

There is another step we can take in getting involved and that is attending school board meetings. Shouldn't we be there when new textbooks and new programs are being discussed? Why is the presence of God missing from our local schools? It is because we have been missing! We also have been playing truant and deserve to explain our absence to our heavenly Father.

When the school board wrestles with a difficult issue, maybe they ask in their own way, "Is there not a prophet of the Lord?" The church can bring the wisdom of God to school board meetings and perhaps affect the lives of students and families alike.

The church has the opportunity and the responsibility to bless the children of our school systems. We must get involved, releasing the hope and potential stored up in our students. We have the spiritual authority and power to destroy the shackles of ignorance, drugs, sex, low self-esteem, and poverty. We must make a choice. Will we sit on the sidelines criticizing, or will we jump in and get involved?

Through Project Impact we work with troubled students in various ways. For suspended students, we go to the schools and pick up the work assigned to them in order to keep them up to pace with the rest of their class. We have classrooms set up with computers and other educational resources needed to get them back on track. Without our intervention, these students might not be able to complete their assignments and would fall even further behind when they returned to school. If someone doesn't intervene, they will be set up for more failure that in the end will lead to anger and violence.

We have worked hand in hand with school administrators eventually returning to their care students who had been suspended for carrying weapons. Many have come from troubled or nonexistent, dysfunctional family backgrounds. Life for them is a struggle just to survive. The trouble at home is then extended to the school grounds and into the classrooms.

Most of the kids act out because of a lack of love and attention. Some of them feel so lost. They reach out for help, but way too often there is no one there to extend a hand and keep them from drowning in despair and hopelessness. With loving care and personal attention we have been able to save these struggling students from being suspended and losing their lives. In the beginning we experienced a unique problem with some of the students. They were intentionally getting suspended so that they would be sent to a place where they could experience love. The program was working.

Many teachers tell us how dramatically their students have been changed. I believe the program has affected not only the students and their families, but also establishes a new atmosphere of hope throughout the schools.

We have proved that love makes a dramatic difference.

Community Government

We also need to tear down the walls that separate the church from the community and city government. Recently our city was preparing to approve a legislative act that would seriously impact all that we were successfully doing in the community. Rather than get angry, we got involved. We brought together many diverse churches in the community. We discussed the issues, and then went as a united front to the city council. We told the council that we simply would not allow them to establish these laws thus furthering the breakdown of the family unit. We sat around the table with elected officials and informed them that we could no longer support them at election time if these laws were passed. They did not pass the new laws.

It is important that we be involved on an ongoing basis, not just when a hot issue comes up. We should participate just as any other citizen. The church can connect and relate with the village government by asking government officials to visit our churches and talk to our congregations. Ask the local leaders to come and share their visions for the city. Do you know what the five-year plan of your city is? Find out where you can position yourself into that plan.

Ask the chief of police to talk to your youth. Ask the candidates of the various political parties who are running for office to come to your church on a Saturday to explain their positions. Some of our members can be trained to help at election time. Although we can't endorse a political party from the pulpit, it is important for our people to know the issues and the problems. Let's get involved in tearing down the walls that separate the church from the community.

Get in the Game!

Church, it is time to get out of the bleachers and into the game. We sit by as observers hollering at the umpire from the stands. The government does something we don't like and we become outraged. The real outrage is that by our silence we allowed it to happen. We can't affect the outcome of the game if we aren't in the game.

Once I threatened to bring food vendors into our Sunday morning services because the people of the congregation were not getting involved. I told them if they were just going to be spectators, we might as well sell hot dogs and popcorn and make some money. They laughed, but I was serious. We need to get into the game if we are to change the score. The villages around our churches ought to have the cleanest streets, the safest and most productive schools, and the best governments. It's time to get off the bench and into the game!

Salt and Light

We have many frustrated and unfulfilled people in the pews of our congregations. They gather for church without any significant purpose. As the Body of Christ we do have purpose and destiny: We are to be salt and light to the village.

> *Ye are the salt of the earth: but if the salt have lost his savour, wherewith shall it be salted? it is thenceforth good for nothing, but to be cast out, and to be trodden under foot of men. Ye are the light of the world. A city that is set on an hill cannot be hid. Neither do men light a candle, and put it under a bushel, but on a candlestick; and it giveth light unto all that are in the house. Let your light so shine before men, that they may see your good works, and glorify your Father which is in heaven (Matthew 5:13-16).*

Salt has an effect upon everything it touches. It is a preservative that prevents the corruption of food and enhances its flavor. The church should be a preserving and flavoring influence in the village. However, we keep our salt in the salt-shaker. We need to get the salt out of the shaker and into the village flavoring it with the love of Jesus Christ.

Jesus also told us we are to be light. Light dispels the darkness. The village authorities stumble in the dark as they look for answers, while they do not even really know the right questions. They ask, "How can we feed and educate the village?" "How can we deal with the drug war that rages in the streets?" We must understand that the real issues are much deeper than these.

It is crucial that we deal with the root causes of these problems: broken families, limited opportunities, and damaged hopes. We must be prepared to reach out and work with the local government of the village. We can no longer afford to hide our light under a bushel of political separation from the civic authorities. We must climb down from the lofty heights of religious superiority and take the flavor and light of the gospel of Jesus Christ into the despair and darkness of the village streets.

It Takes a Church to Raise a Village!

Endnote

1. Treasure House publishing style normally capitalized the word *Church* when it refers to the universal Body of Christ. In this chapter, *church* refers to a local organization; therefore, it is lowercased.

Chapter Seven

If you see in any given situation only what everybody else can see, you can be said to be so much a representative of your culture that you are a victim of it.

S.I. Hayakawa
U.S. scholar

Chapter Seven

Funding the Vision

And said unto the king...why should not my countenance be sad, when the city, the place of my fathers' sepulchres, lieth waste, and the gates thereof are consumed with fire? Then the king said unto me, For what dost thou make request?....Moreover I said unto the king...let letters be given me to the governors beyond the river, that they may convey me over till I come into Judah; and a letter unto Asaph the keeper of the king's forest, that he may give me timber to make beams for the gates of the palace which appertained to the house, and for the wall of the city, and for the house that I shall enter into. And the king granted me, according to the good hand of my God upon me (Nehemiah 2:3-4,7-8).

Jerusalem lay in ruins. Those who remained in the city lived in dread and despair amidst the devastation of a past glory. What was once the glorious center of a blessed nation had become little more than a howling waste—its very name a parable of destruction. Nehemiah, empowered by the political power of his day and encouraged by the vision God had given him, set out to rebuild this desolate city. The vision for restoration must begin by removing the debris of broken walls and rebuilding the desolation of burning gates.

This biblical story taken out of Jewish antiquity reminds us of the reality of today's inner cities. Streets once lined with businesses and alive with commercial activity are now reduced to empty storefronts and despondent people. This pitiful portrait gives us an idea of the pain in Nehemiah's heart as he examined the condition of his beloved Jerusalem. Do we have the same profound passionate burden for our cities as Nehemiah did? Do we have the resources to transform our vision into a reality? It is going to take more than a vision and a burden to change our cities—it's going to take financial support!

Finances are waiting to be released for Kingdom purposes. We can't fry enough chickens, bake enough cakes, or sell enough used clothing to do the work that God has commissioned us to do. We must find the money to finance the vision. Somebody must pay for the shoes that go on the feet of those who carry the good news of the gospel (see Is. 52:7). We must start fighting through writing—by learning how to apply for grants. (See Appendix B.)

Financing the vision is the issue before us. Where do we find the cash to rebuild the waste places of our beloved cities? How do we effectively budget that money for financing creative projects that will transform our neighborhoods? From Nehemiah's day to the present day, these are the ABC's of funding a successful project: *Accountability*, *Budgeting*, and *Character*.

Accountability

What do we mean by *accountability*? Accountability simply means that we do what we say we are going to do. If you send me to the store with money to buy a loaf of bread, then I need to return with a loaf of bread, a receipt, and your change. Those things must add up to the total of what was given to me. I must make an accounting for any other use or discrepancy. The first step then to being accountable is to know what our end goal is and how to reach it. In other words, if we expect someone to contribute finances towards a project, we must be able to communicate a clear and concise *vision* for the work.

Vision

Before we can begin to talk about resources for building a ministry, we need to know what we are called to build. We can't expect anyone to help us build something without telling them what we are going to build. Would we go to a bank and ask them for a loan to build a house before showing them that we have a blueprint and a contractor? Of course we wouldn't.

Funding the Vision

We must therefore draft a blueprint for the agencies we hope to create and financially subsidize. That blueprint is our vision.

To determine what your congregation should be involved in, ask yourself, "What do I see?" It's not an issue of just doing anything. We must specifically know what we are called to do. Jesus knew where to minister because He looked to see where His Father was working. Jesus said, "Verily, verily, I say unto you, The Son can do nothing of Himself, but what He seeth the Father do: for what things soever He doeth, these also doeth the Son likewise" (Jn. 5:19). Jesus did not work to keep Himself occupied or to create a positive image for His ministry. He had the spiritual perceptiveness that enabled Him to peek into the spiritual realm and determine what the Father was doing. This spiritual discernment provided the direction for His work.

The apostle Paul makes that same emphasis. He refers to it as a "sphere." "But we will not boast beyond our measure, but within the measure of the sphere which God apportioned to us as a measure, to reach even as far as you" (2 Cor. 10:13 NAS). God has apportioned to us a space that determines our area of work. God defines this *sphere* by introducing a passion into our spirit and imparting a vision to meet that need. We must never forget that the work is God's and that He is merely inviting us to become involved in His own work. Like Jesus and Paul, we must look to see where God is working and at His invitation join in with Him.

Our Love School started as a result of *seeing* the need of children who had no meals on the weekends. The need was always there, but in a special moment in time the Lord opened our eyes to see those starving kids and empowered us to meet that need. In the same way, we were inspired to start a literacy program. All of this happened because we *saw* hungry children and illiterate persons. Our congregation has grown from a few people to more than one thousand because we learned how to respond in faith and compassion to the needs around us.

Each new work or agency started by our church was the result of a need that we saw in our precious community. Don't start a drug rehab program or a literacy program just because that seems to be the fashionable and religious thing to do. You need to find out what God is doing in your community and get on board with His plan. I like to consider myself a need-creator. I spend time identifying needs in the community, then begin to discover resourceful and substantial ways to minister to those needs.

> *We must have faith to believe that He will finance the vision that He gives us. If He can get it through us, He will get it to us.*

You must remember that the Lord will provide the seed for where He leads. We must have faith to believe that He will finance the vision that He gives us. If He can get it through us, He will get it to us.

Just as Nehemiah painted a clear picture of his calling for the king, we must also provide a clear vision to those who will follow us and those who will support us. Nehemiah knew what he was called to do, what resources were needed, and how long it would take to do the job. That's a vision! Having a clear vision is the first part of our *accountability*.

Integrity

The next key part of accountability is *integrity*. Integrity is the integration of what we *say* into what we *do.* It is the merger of word and work. The reason that Nehemiah so easily gained the favor of a powerful king was because of his own display of personal integrity. As the king's cupbearer, Nehemiah literally held the king's life in his own hands. If the king could trust Nehemiah with his life, he could surely trust him

102

with a few timbers needed to build some gates. If we are to find the finances to raise the village, we must have a public testimony of integrity.

I heard about an archbishop of the Catholic Church in California who walked into a financial resource meeting and demanded six million dollars for his agency. He received the money despite other competing programs. Why? Because of *integrity*. The archbishop always did what he said he was going to do. He produced results. They didn't give him money because he was a nice person or had good intentions, but because he was successful in his public service. It is a little known fact that the government gives more money each year to the Catholic Church than to any other charitable organization. In 1994 the Catholic Church received 218 million dollars because they met the needs of the village. The Catholic Church has always had a positive reputation of establishing not only churches, but also hospitals and schools. They have dealt with many needs of the community involving body, mind, and spirit. The government does not tell them how to conduct Mass, but they give them authority to educate, counsel, and deal with other needs. They continue to give them money because the Catholic Church faithfully does what they say they will do. They have integrity! The Spirit-filled Church must do the same. The Catholic Church has the authority and the money from the government because they ask for it, and then they prove themselves worthy of it. We must prove ourselves worthy by faithfully carrying out what we promise to do.

Our church has experienced the same power of trust with our local officials. We have been so faithful in how we have performed our work that they now notify us when the government is going to make funding available. It is because we do what we say we are going to do. And when they send an auditor over, we can prove it.

Organization

Another part of our accountability is *organization*. Church-related agencies come under the watchful eye of auditors. It is imperative that our ministries are always "audit ready." Invariably, there are strings attached to money, and the main string here is that we keep good financial records. If the government invests taxpayers' money in our vision, we better be able to prove that we are effectively and accurately handling these public funds. Accurate records demonstrate a good faith use of finances and are essential if we expect to get more funding. Proper handling of public funds lays the foundation to receive additional financial public support for the dreams that God gives us.

Although Project Impact is new on the block in Dayton, we maintain some of the best records of any agency in the city. When we meet with other agencies, they mention the accuracy and quality of our financial records. Because we maintain good and accurate records, we don't have to scramble at the last minute to pull our information together. Without fear or wonder, we open our books at any moment to the auditor. If money is not spent wisely, it reflects poorly on the government as well as the agency. Therefore, when the government has money to invest in the community, they will remember those who have been responsible.

"A" is for accountability in our *vision*, our *integrity*, and our *organization*. Once we have presented a clear picture of what we want to do and understand how we will do it, we can move on to "B," which stands for *budgeting*.

Budgeting

All the resources we need to fund our God-given projects are available to us both inside and outside the church. Where do they come from and how do we get them? These resources include the government at every level, charitable trusts, large corporations, and a variety of other sources. (See Appendix C on funding sources.)

Resources Outside the Church

One of the first things to establish in your ministry is a CFO (chief financial officer). This person will be in charge of matching needs with funding. If you are serious about raising the village, this position could be full time. There are millions of dollars at the disposal of "faith-based organizations" to rebuild communities. It is also true that millions of dollars go unclaimed simply because the church does not know where to find the money. We have received phone calls saying, "We are about to send back $40,000 nobody has applied for. Do you want it?" You don't have to ask me twice.

We need to be actively involved in searching out the needs of our community and seeing how we can best invest the resources that the Lord provides. The money is out there. If we don't use it for the Kingdom, it will go somewhere else. We, like Nehemiah, have to be brave and go ask the king (government, etc.). In fact, if we have made the need and vision clear, our funding sources will come to us and do the asking just as the king asked Nehemiah, "How can I help?"

We must also learn how to communicate using the same terminology employed by the government and other funding sources. Grant proposals must be written in the proper language. The current politically correct and spiritually appropriate word in the country is "family." At Project Impact we deal with a whole range of family problems as we teach on the whole range of "family values." So when they hand us a grant form, we talk in terms of the "family," not Bible studies. It is not necessary to tell a funding source that Jesus is the basis for all our teaching. They already know that we are a faith-based organization. Funding sources are interested in the product, not necessarily the process. We have written a proposal for 3.5 million dollars to build a family resource center. Although the government will never build us a church, they just might build us a gym. The government will not build you a baptismal, but they could give you computers. We have more than 30 computers on site and I don't think we paid for any of them. We can have church in the gym! Are we more interested in religion or results? We need to learn to speak the language of our funding sources. Didn't our Lord teach us that we should be as wise as serpents and as harmless as doves?

Most churches do not realize the opportunities for ministry in their own communities. For example, they look at government housing projects and only see the danger and problems that they create, instead of considering the many opportunities and millions of dollars available to meet the unique needs in these communities. We can sit around complaining that government misuses money, or we can make a decision that we will learn how to tap into those resources for the purposes of God.

In addition to receiving contracts for truancy programs as well as schoolwork study programs, Project Impact accepts government funding to provide many other contract services related to the housing projects. We serve the Dayton Metropolitan Housing Projects for which the government has given us a large sum annual contract to minister to the families there. We should not overlook any ministry or funding source that the Lord reveals to us.

If your pastoral staff are involved in the oversight of the agencies you operate, it is possible to fund those positions with government money. We have 22 full-time staff at Project Impact and an operating budget of $1.5 million per year, half of which is supplied by government funding. Many on our staff have dual roles. They may serve in the agency during the day and as youth ministers on weekends. The Church needs to start thinking in new ways. We should be discovering how the Lord wants to accomplish His ministry in our villages.

Many sources of funding are fed up with the larger agencies they have supported in the past. Larger agencies are not able to produce results because of their own high administrative costs. These sources are now looking for smaller agencies to fund because of their ability to produce better results. The time is ripe for church-related agencies to do the work of the Kingdom and minister to community needs in ways that no one else can. This is a time for us to move outside the walls of our churches.

Another source of funding is the United Way and their "donor option." The donor has the opportunity to determine how his money will be spent. He fills out a card at work, consenting to a payroll deduction; then 100 percent of the donated money is given to the organization of his choice. We get thousands of dollars every year from the United Way—and the donor does not even have to be a member of our congregation. We need to get the word out to our families. Money can be directly taken from their paycheck and given to a church simply by filling out a card.

We need to learn how to ask for money without fear of rejection. The worst anyone can say is "no." I am not afraid of rejection. I had cancer in 1985 and a massive stroke in 1993. The word *no* does not bother me. We have been turned down a few times, but we just keep asking.

We have asked a well-known restaurant chain to give us one of their buildings. They've rejected our request. But I keep calling them back and telling them that I need the building for a job-training center for which the government will give the money to operate. Sooner or later they will find out that we mean business—Kingdom business!

If you see a building standing empty, find out who owns it and don't be afraid to ask for it. If you discover a source that is willing to give money to do some village-raising work, don't be afraid to ask for it. The worst they can say is no. "You have not because you ask not!" Let them know what you are doing. Put your vision on paper, and begin to circulate that vision. (See Appendix A on proposal checklist.)

We are a nine-year-old congregation and we operate three buildings: a family building, a family life center, and an office building. The office building was empty when we found that the owners were looking for a non-profit organization to offer it to. Most visitors can't believe that this beautiful facility is owned and operated by a local church. It was given to us and all we had to do was pay off a $10,000 balance. I'll take an office building on those terms any time.

Pastors need to put down the Wall Street Journal and pick up the Chronicle of Philanthropy, a monthly publication that lists millions of available dollars. The money is out there. We just have to find it and then ask for it. We must cease spending so much time working on our financial portfolio and start looking for available money to invest in the village.

I attended the first national conference on Black Philanthropy in Philadelphia. There were many large corporations represented such as the Ford Foundation, the Kellogg Foundation, and the Kresge Foundation. The conference highlighted five black congregations who were serving in powerfully effective community work and explained how these congregations were funding those programs. The figures were in the millions of dollars. The churches highlighted were of various denominations: Baptist, Lutheran, and Methodist, along with Bishop Charles Blake's congregation.

Funding the Vision

The National Congress of Black Churches has received six million dollars from the Lilly Foundation to rebuild churches that were burned down, and they are seeking an additional six million dollars. Foundations, such as the Lilly Foundation, are looking for grassroots organizations because they are producing the results. Newspapers are now reporting how the church is coming into an effective place of ministry in the community.

There must be an end to the competitive spirit that sometimes exists among churches and ministries. Everyone wants the credit for something done in the name of the Lord Jesus. This spirit will cease to be a reality in the church when they come under the lordship of Jesus Christ. The fruit of our labor is not honor from the world, but lives changed forever by the power of God demonstrated by the Church.

There are more than enough resources to go around to do the work of raising the village. Some ministries keep funding sources a secret for fear that a competing ministry will get some money or do a more impressive work. I have come to the opposite conclusion. I give out the names of any resource that I find. They do not belong to me. Freely I have received, so freely I give.

Resources in the Church

Some of the most precious resources are sitting right in the pews of the church. In a previous chapter, we briefly spoke about the need to turn beggars into blessers with the turning of the hand. Along with this, the Church needs to teach on the principles of tithing and giving. How many people in our congregations struggle with their own financial problems because they have not released their finances to the Lord? How many in the village are not being ministered to, on account of unavailable funds, because your congregation is not being taught how to give? In many church services offering time is seen as some kind of intermission when people slip out the back, go to the restroom, or visit with someone. This should not be. The people are deprived, and God is robbed.

Launch a treasure hunt in your own congregation to find your "jewels in the pews." You should be discovering the skills and abilities in your church that can be translated into the work of the Kingdom of God. Create a survey sheet that identifies these skilled positions in your church. This house inventory will be critical to forming a team that can fulfill the vision. You can motivate the congregation by sharing the power and potential of your vision with them. Tell them what you envision in the community. Many of these "jewels" are bored with church and are waiting to be invited into something that they find personally challenging and fundamentally significant.

The leadership of the Church cannot handle all the work of the ministry. Every member of the Body should have a function and a focus for their ministry. That function and focus must be worked out in the context of a unified effort. God has designed His Body to operate as a team—a corporate ministry. Jesus utilized the practical skills of the various members of His first ministry team. He was able to redeem and transform their worldly skills into ones that would bring profit to the Kingdom of God. In one instance Jesus said, "Follow Me, and I will make you fishers of men" (Mt. 4:19b). Today we might say, "Join us and we will make you apostolic accountants or Kingdom carpenters or even loving lawyers." What skills do you have lying around your house that could be incorporated into the purposes of God? Are there people with communication and legal skills that can write a grant proposal? Are there attorneys who can offer legal counsel? Are there good listeners who can form the base for a counseling ministry? Many of our secular skills can be translated into Kingdom usefulness. We must help them all to become "fishers of men."

At Revival Ministries we have already been involved in converting worldly skills into Kingdom skills. For example, a retired schoolteacher, who was a reading specialist in her professional life, has been instrumental in the development of our own literacy program, as she cheerfully shares her talents and training. She has converted her profession into a Kingdom ministry. We have senior citizens with renewed youthful zeal because they have found new purpose by serving in various ministries. Their lives are being transformed as they are transforming the lives of others.

There is a story about some young men in Russia who were on their way to a forbidden Bible study. They came upon some KGB agents who stopped them and asked them where they were going. At first the men were frightened at what might happen to them if they revealed the truth. But the Holy Spirit moved on them to tell the KGB agents that their Elder Brother had died and they were going to a reading of His last will and testament. The KGB sent them on their way. Later, after the Bible study concluded, they returned full of the joy of the Lord and once again encountered the KGB men. The KGB asked them, "Well how did the reading go?" The young men said, "Great! He left us everything!" What a powerful story and how true! Indeed, our Elder Brother has left us resources and everything we need to raise up the village.

Character

Perhaps the most important facet of our fund-raising efforts is *character*. As a church agency we must not compromise our conviction for cash. Don't try to get more money than what your program needs. Don't try to grow your program to a level higher than the needed funds. If your ministry needs

$30,000, don't ask for $50,000. We must be responsible in our actions and demonstrate Christian character in everything we do. Stay within your vision and abilities, and you will discover that you will have more credibility the next time you return to the well asking for more.

We should not disguise the fact that we are Christian. It will be an open invitation for secular officials to come observe what we are doing. We have had judges, commissioners, and other civil authorities, as well as school principals come to Project Impact meetings as well as visit our church services. They have attended our graduations and sat under the influence of our prayer. They know that we pray with the children. They are aware that we minister in our various programs without forcing religion on them. We don't have to present Bible lessons with every job-training seminar. We will "re-present" Him by our consistent character and compassionate communications.

We will be remembered more for our character than our brilliant program strategies. It is the character of Jesus Christ that must be on display in everything we do. We must establish the ministry upon the character of Christ. All that we do must bring Him glory and honor.

As you move forward in establishing your ministry to raise the village, remember the ABC's: *Accountability, Budget,* and *Character*.

Our Elder Brother has left us everything we need to raise the village. Let us raise it together in His name and for His glory.

It Takes a Church to Raise a Village!

Chapter Eight

Lord, make me a channel of thy peace
that where there is hatred, I may bring love;
that where there is wrong, I may bring the spirit of forgiveness;
that where there is discord, I may bring harmony;
that where there is error, I may bring truth;
that where there is doubt, I may bring faith;
that where there is despair, I may bring hope;
that where there is shadows, I may bring light;
that where there is sadness, I may bring joy.
Lord, grant that I may seek rather to comfort than to be comforted;
to understand, than to be understood;
to love, than to be loved.
For it is by self-forgetting that one finds.
It is by forgiving that one is forgiven.
It is by dying that one awakens to Eternal Life.

St. Francis of Assisi

Chapter Eight

It Takes a Church to Raise a Village

It Takes a Church to Raise a Village, but what kind of a Church will it take?

There was a time in history when a beautiful young woman arose to the aid of her nation. Her people were captive in a pagan land, subject to an ungodly world system, living under a sentence of death. The young maiden responsible for saving this nation from an evil establishment happened to be the bride of a great king.

Likewise, the Church, living in a pagan world system, is the Bride of the King of kings. The Church who raises the village will be the one who most resembles the bride of that ancient king. We can learn much from her in our efforts to save the village. Her name was Esther. Unfortunately, there was also another queen...

The Esther Church

There was once a queen in the far-off and ancient kingdom of Persia. Her name was Vashti, which meant "beautiful." And so she was. She was adorned in expensive clothes and lived in a most extravagant dwelling place. Neglecting her duty as the bride of the king and forgetting her life was to please him and be responsive to his call, she instead spent most of her time in front of a mirror admiring herself. She was more concerned with her appearance than with obedience.

Yes, she was beautiful, but her beauty was wasted on herself. She made sure that she looked attractive and smelled pleasant, but for her sake alone. One day the king sent his seven servants to summon her, "but the queen Vashti refused...the king" (Esther 1:12). She refused to be moved by his calling. Her arrogance not only enraged the king, but caused offense to the whole kingdom as well. Experts of the law advised the king to search the land far and wide for someone else to replace the one who was captivated by her own splendor. The king was pleased with this recommendation and decided to give her estate to another bride who was "better than she" (Esther 1:19b).

A maiden was found. Her name was "Hadassah," the word for *myrtle*. A myrtle is an aromatic, humble plant with beautiful foliage, which produces an edible fruit. Its leaves are also used to provide shelter for pilgrims. Her Persian name was Esther, meaning "the star"...a name associated with heavenly beauty.

She was an orphan of Israel. As an orphan she had no ties that would create rival affection or misplaced loyalty. She was totally available for the king. She was not caught up in politics; she was only caught up in the king.

Esther was taken to the king's house for a time of preparation. She was immersed in oil and precious perfumes for a year, six months of myrrh and six months of sweet fragrances, so that all traces of the world would be removed. Myrrh is the scent of humility, which was necessary before she could bring pleasure to the king. When her preparation was complete, she was taken to the king. He loved her more than all the others and she obtained favor in his eyes as well as all of those with whom she had contact. A crown was placed upon her head. She was as responsive to the king as he was delighted in her presence.

Esther was more than a pretty face in the court of the king. She was devoted to her own Jewish people. When there came a threat against them, she was not afraid to adorn herself with royal robes and approach the king on their behalf. She knew that it was for just *"such a time as this"* that she had attained royalty. (See Esther 4:14.)

Her position to the king was not merely for her own comfort but as an intercessor for the people of God. Knowing that there was an evil plot to destroy her people, she risked her own life by going into the king's presence uninvited, to secure their safety. Esther used her own position of grace with the king to release the power that would destroy the plans of the enemy.

In this brief summary of the life of Esther, we uncover a model for the Church who will raise the village. If we are to raise the village, then we will reflect these same attributes.

The Church who will raise the village will be...

...An Orphaned Church

The orphaned Church is one who moves beyond the bounds of denominationalism. This is not to say that she cannot be part of a denomination, only that she will not be bound by anything other than her desire to serve the purpose of God, her King. When a woman gets married there is sometime a temptation to draw back to her original home and family. Her birth family may be more comfortable and familiar to her. But a bride must leave the house of her family and be separated unto her husband. She no longer serves the purpose of her family; she now makes a home with her groom. She can only obey one of them. It should be her husband.

In the same way the Church who is challenged to raise the village must make obedience to the purpose of God a higher priority than the perpetuation of the customs and rites of her denomination. She may be Baptist, Lutheran, or Pentacostal, but her first priority is to serve the King, not her denominational headquarters. She is to be involved in the redemption of the community in which she lives. She must be a Bride with sleeves rolled up and ready to serve.

She must be prepared to work alongside people of other denominations and traditions. She cannot look at the other maidens in the King's house with disdain or envy. They all serve the same King. The Church who raises the village will be separated from the system, an orphaned Church.

Along a similar line, the village Church will be...

...A Purified Church

For six months Esther and the other maidens were soaked in oil of myrrh. Myrrh was a precious scent used for, among other things, the anointing of bodies. It is a sign of self-death— a sign of humility. She must be purified in her *attitude*. The Church must be purified of her own pride and arrogance. We get so involved in the achievements we accomplish or the doctrines we declare that we forget that our only purpose is to please the King.

She must be purified in her *conduct*. The Bride of Christ must also be purified of the stink of the world. She needs to live in a strong personal relationship with the Lord. She is *in* the world but not *of* the world as Jesus said. (see Jn. 17:14). Some in the Church have gotten so close to the world that they retain the stink of it. Preachers have fallen into disgrace with extramarital affairs and financial scandals. The greatest scandal of all is that the village crumbles while the Church remains inside the royal powder room admiring her beauty in her own self-created mirror. To some the Bride of Christ has become the punch line of late night TV jokes. The Bride has not been purified. She has not lived under the lordship of her Master, the King.

The greatest scandal of all is that the village crumbles while the Church remains inside the royal powder room admiring her beauty in her own self-created mirror.

The Church who is capable of raising the village must also be purified in her *motives*. Who is getting the glory for what she does? Whose purpose does she serve? Whose name is being exalted? The motive of the Bride must be to give glory to the Bridegroom. She does not work to impress others in the Body of Christ or the community with her numbers or her genius.

And the Bride will work in the anointing of the King. Everything she does will be saturated with the fragrance of the

King. She may never mention the King's name as she undertakes her ministry alongside the village, but there will be no mistaking *who* she belongs to. She carries the fragrance of the King into the dead and littered streets of a dying village. And everything that she touches retains that sweet smell. The world will ask, "What is that perfume you're wearing?" The Bride spreads the aroma of the King's house without preaching a sermon or handing out a gospel tract.

The Church who raises the village must be an orphaned Church, and a purified Church, and she must also be...

...An Available Church

The great downfall of Vashti, the king's first queen, was that she was so consumed with herself that she could not respond to the king. She ceased being a bride and became a queen. The Church who effectively raises the village will be a Church who is responsive to the call of the King. The King will send forth his sevenfold Spirit and summon her to Himself and she will answer...not just for a time of rapture in the King's arms, but to live her life for His purposes. She will see the needs in the village and devote herself to them. She may be called to teach them, to read to them, or take them to work. Whatever the calling, she will be *available*.

The church cannot remain aloof from the needs of the village. Vashti thought the banquet of the king was beneath her dignity, so she ignored it. This was not only an affront to the great king of Persia, but to the nation. When there is an obvious need in the village and the "Vasti Church" is content to stay in her royal powder room, it is an affront to our King. We must not be enchanted with our own splendor while we ignore the village around us.

The Church who raises the village will be one who hears the sounds of weeping from the abortion clinic, to the school yard, to the empty bellies of hungry children. The Church who raises the village will also be...

...A Gracious Church

It was said of Esther that she did not demand anything from the king. She was one who knew she lived in the grace of her sovereign lord. So must we. We are not in a position to judge those to whom we are called to minister. We stand in the grace of God and we are called to extend that same grace to the village. Esther was not a spoiled, pampered delicacy isolated from the masses of her own people. The Church who will raise the village will conduct herself with grace and humility of mind in the village. She will require no special treatment. She will not consider herself to be better than those around her in the village.

The Church must earn the favor of those around her by adhering to the same conditions and rules that they do. We must complete our paperwork better than everyone else. We must be competitive in the services we offer. We must do a first-class job and be effective in all that we put our hands to. We work in the name of Jesus Christ whether or not we ever speak it. The quality of our work and the manner in which we perform will speak His name more loudly than any sermon we could preach on a street corner.

We must be a gracious Church, but we must also be...

...A Praying Church

The Church and the village have a common enemy. And he comes to steal, kill, and destroy us all. His name is satan. There are those liberal cultural Christians who do not believe that there is a satan, and that is just fine with him. He laughs all the way to the abortion clinic. He is delighted to pull the village down around his feet. He wants to take as many as he can with him to his reservation in that lake of fire. He is a liar telling the village that there is no hope...no way out except to get high on dope. He is a lion roaring about the streets of our villages bringing fear to all that pay attention to him.

Our common enemy is actively seeking our destruction. He hates God and he hates the village. He especially hates the Church. He has conspired to bring the village down, to wipe out the seed of the next generation and to destroy God's people. However, we have the advantage—we are married to the King!

But just like Esther, we must put on our royal robes of Christ's righteousness and go into the presence of the King with petitions. We must ask the King for favor over the enemy. We are called into His presence for this very purpose. His Spirit groans within us carrying the burden of the village.

The Church who raises the village must be a praying Church. We must not be afraid to enter the King's chambers with our petitions on behalf of the village. As we enter with petitions, the King will give us all we need to do the work. He will empower us with His presence and prepare the way for us. As Esther's king did, He will say. "All that you have asked for has been done. What else do you need?" (See Esther 9:12-13.) It is the power of the King that will destroy the minions of satan.

The Church who raises the village will be a *praying* Church, but she will also be...

...A Wise Church

Esther knew the plot and plan of the enemy and she took the battle to him. She laid a trap with her own diligence and character. So will we. We must be wise to the devices of the enemy. Not only do we need to have diligently prayed to address the problems of the village, but we also need to read and study as much as we can. Our people must be wise in the ways and the language of the streets. But they must also be qualified to address the problems. Two and two must still add up to four, even for the Church. The laws of time and space will not be altered just because we are the Church. The Church needs common sense and prudence to meet needs in the village. We cannot walk around on the clouds if we desire to minister on the streets. Once the Lord has pointed out the area in which we are to work, we need to seek qualification to do the work. The state is not going to give out money to those who do not have the qualifications to spend it.

Esther knew how to catch Haman in his own schemes. We must know how to work the system and use it to our advantage as well as that of the village. If we are going to put the devil out of business, we must be better than he is. We must beat him at his own game. Do you want to get rid of the porn shops in your village? Then train your people to operate respectable businesses to replace them. Do you want to extract the wealth of the village for the work of the King? Then work to raise the level of education and expectation of the people in your church and village. People do not want to be poor. They just expect they will always be poor and they fulfill their own expectations. That is the devil's plan. We let him sell it on every village street corner. It is a lie! The only way to raise the village is to raise the expectation of the villagers.

All the wealth of the king was available to Esther. Anything that we need is available to us if we will follow the plan we have outlined. If we do what we are called to do in the way that honors the King, the government and foundations will ask, *"What else do you need?"* They will come looking for us!

The Church must be *orphaned, pure, available, gracious, praying* and *wise*, but we must also be...

...a Church of Destiny

Esther knew that it was *"for such a time as this"* that she had attained her position. She knew that she had a destiny to fulfill. There was something bigger than her own existence. She had attained her position for nothing less than the salvation of her people.

Church, we have been raised up "for such a time as this." It is obvious even to the most liberal politicians that the government cannot meet the needs of our villages. We have the people and the will. Now all we need is the money and the skill.

The Church who raises the village will not be busy doing her own thing. She will answer the summons of the King putting her own life aside to deal with the problems of her people, the village. She will be the one to raise the village.

Those from among you will rebuild the ancient ruins; you will raise up the age-old foundations; and you will be called the repairer of the breach, the restorer of the streets in which to dwell (Isaiah 58:12 NAS).

It Takes a Church to Raise a Village!

Appendix A

Proposal Checklist

Proposal Checklist

A complete proposal should include the following information in the order stated.

- Proposal Cover sheet. All items must be completed.
- Concise history of the organization, with an overview of current programs and activities.
- Copy of the Internal Revenue Service letter stating the organization is a tax-exempt public charity.
- Statement from the organization's board authorizing the request and agreeing to carry out the project if funded.
- Description of the problem or need to be met by the project.
- Detailed description of the project including goals (strategies), measurable objectives, and timetable.
- Names and qualifications of persons responsible for carrying out the program.
- Detailed project budget and budget narrative, including income sources and expenditures; a list of other requests for funding, including those pending or approved.
- Evidence of financial condition. Letter from CPA or last audit.
- Plan for continuing the project once Foundation funding ends.
- Plan for evaluating the project.
- Letters recommending the project and other relevant supporting material such as reports, brochures, or news articles. People affected by the problem/clients & clients' family.

Applicants should submit an original and three copies of their completed proposal.

Appendix B

How to Write a Proposal

How to Write a Proposal

Before You Write

Depending on the Funding Source Application Guidelines, the following information will be requested. Take the time to assemble the information, place in sets and file. Only send what they request.

- 501 © (3) letter from IRS
- List of Board of Directors — names, addresses, phone numbers
- Copy of most recent audit
- List of Advisory Council members
- Map of target area
- Demographics of target population
- Resumes and job descriptions of current and proposed staff
- Sample budgets
- Sample budget narrative
- Letter requesting letters of support and list of requestees
- History of organization: programs, awards, positive information
- Minutes of board meetings and attendance numbers
- Future funding statement
- Evaluation statement

Appendix C

Support Information

R.I.S.E.
Raising Internal Self-Esteem
A program of the
Prevention Services Division
A Division of
Project IMPACT-Dayton, Inc.
"Equipping Youth and their Families for Success"

Program Overview

Mission Statement

To address the special needs of female offenders.

Because female delinquents are outnumbered by boys in the juvenile justice system, and because girl offenders may seem less dangerous to society, the needs of young ladies have gone largely unaddressed. However, more young ladies are entering the system. Some are committing more violent offenses, such as assault. Gender-specific programming offers a way to tailor juvenile justice services specifically to the needs of young ladies.

Population Served

Female offenders on probation, ages 11 through 15 who are adjudicated, unruly or delinquent, and are enrolled in school.

Services/Activities

Intake and Assessment, Female Adolescence Development, Academic Assistance, Leadership Development, Mentors and Parenting/Family Education

Programming consists of three modules:

Intake & Assessment	Intensive Day Treatment (8-week session)	Aftercare (6-month program)
Assessment Case Management Services	Case Management Evening & Weekend Activities Parenting/Family Education	Case Management Services Evening & Weekend Activities (includes periodic involvement of parents) Mentoring Developmental Activities

The program, which consists of three modules, targets delinquent and unruly females between the ages of 11-15 years, and is implemented over an eight-month period.

137

It Takes a Church to Raise a Village

Young Parent Support Program
A Program of
Prevention Services
A Division of Project IMPACT-Dayton

Services
- Support System
- Training
- Home Visits
- Case Management
- Referrals
- Incentives

Class Topics
- Goals
- Child Maltreatment/ Abuse
- Child Development
- Anger/Stress/Time Management
- Single Parenting
- Money Management
- Communication
- Discipline Methods
- Family Relationships
- Sex and Dating

Criteria
- Ages 18-24
- Custody of at least one (1) child between age two (2) and five (5)
- Parent cannot have an open case with the Children's Services Bureau

Supported by
- Lutheran Social Services
- Ohio Wellness Block Grant
- Ohio Children's Trust Fund

For More Information, Contact
Project IMPACT-Dayton
115 East Third Street
Fourth Floor
(937) 222-LOVE phone
(937) 222-4640 fax

TEN IMPORTANT ELEMENTS FOR CHURCH-SPONSORED COMMUNITY-BASED ORGANIZATIONS

1. Write down the vision-mission statement. Set forth short-term and long-term goals.

2. Staff and volunteers need to have commitment and a heart for the ministry.

3. Prepare a survey for your congregation. (There are "jewels in the pews.") Find out what's in the house.

4. Interact with your community in three areas: (1) needs, (2) problems, (3) leadership.

5. Make yourselves visible in the community. (Attend community meetings, prepare newsletters, conduct special days.)

6. Make your organization an independent corporation. (Separate 501 © (3) designation.)

7. If possible, a separate freestanding facility. (People tend to come to an agency facility vs. a church building.)

8. Contact the local United Way and enroll your organization for Donor Option opportunities.

9. Investigate all the funding opportunities in your community including local municipalities, housing authorities, as well as in-kind opportunities.

10. Faith, Faith, Faith, Faith, Faith, Faith, Faith, Faith!! Faith for every area including faith and more faith.

CHURCH ADMINISTRATION

Church Administration is the foundation for biblical accountability and credibility. This manual shares practical suggestions, insights and wisdom for effective church administration. It has been designed for you to take back to your local church and implement, and/or motivate you to enhance your current practices. For many churches, church administration is a part-time or volunteer financial secretary whose sole responsibility is to pay the monthly bills. The counting and the banking of the offerings is handled by the Head Deacon or Trustee President. This model may be effective for a congregation whose membership is 25 people or less with no outreach programs but it is hardly the organizational structure you will need in place to handle the outreach and discipleship activities of the harvest of souls God is sending into the Church. With growth and additional responsibility, we must set God's House in order to effectively support God's will.

CHURCH AGENCY DEVELOPMENT

God wants His Church to possess the land and win the lost for Christ. He is calling for us to build the Kingdom of God. God wants the Church to go forth with the promises He has given and establish His covenant in the earth. The Lord has given many a "burning" in their hearts to do a work for Him. However, circumstances, finances and naysayers have hindered many from advancing the Kingdom. God is saying that we have delayed long enough. We must believe Him and receive the provision He has given us. *Church Agency Development* is an opportunity whose time has come, and the time is NOW. Arise, Church, and be the AGENCY through which the power of God is exerted for the DEVELOPMENT of His Kingdom to manifest His glory.

This manual will provide churches with an overview on how to develop, operate and staff a church-sponsored agency. Through this manual, you will leave with the essential tools needed to begin the basic steps of creating a community-based organization. This manual will teach you 1. how to develop a church-sponsored agency. 2. how to establish a Board of Directors. 3. how to develop an agency plan, budget, and personnel policies.

GRANT WRITING & FUNDING SOURCES

This manual will help churches and religious agencies get started in the process of grant writing and seeking potential sources of funding for their outreach efforts. The manual will teach you: 1. understanding the preparation for the proposal. 2. how to actually write a grant proposal and position your project for support. 3. how to determine what is a viable project and begin the process of seeking private funds.

LEGAL AND BUDGETING

Is it time? Is it time for the Body of Christ to come forth and claim the land? Is it time? Is it time for the Body of Christ to render liberty and justice through Christ Jesus? IS it time? Is it time for the Body of Christ to come together in one accord to make a difference in every aspect of peoples' lives? This course is a small session into the law. However, the session is not a session on "the law" that the world would have for us. This is a session about the law that God has ordained for each of us who rightly belong to Him and are inspired and fired-up to do the work of the ministry. For it is that law that fails not and never changes, and that works to go in and possess the land; to do those things that will bring glory and honor to His name. That is the law God has for us.

Support Information

SEIZE THE MOMENT

Social conditions are so distressing that society is saying, "Help me any way you can. " They don't care if you pray, preach or play; just produce results and they produce funds. They want the Church to assist them; and the wonderful thing is, that you don't have to give up being "sanctified to be qualified" for funding to help you meet the needs of your community.

The information in this manual is the result of several decades of accumulated wisdom, faith and application of knowledge. On its pages you'll find information that will assist you in increasing the financial capabilities of your outreach and local church ministry. As you read this material, we invite you, the minister or church leader, to join us and tap into the financial reservoir of the world, that has been laid up for the people of God. So in Jesus' name, open your eyes and your spirit, and experience the abundance that is in the land. If you do so, you'll discover that it is truly a great day for the Body of Christ. You'll also agree that there's no better time than the present to *Seize the Moment* and establish the Kingdom of God.

LOVE SCHOOL

This manual tells "how to" find and reach children 6-12 years of age in disadvantaged neighborhoods. Includes ½ day schedule of activities, resources needed along with enrollment and volunteer forms for a Saturday Enrichment Outreach Program. Good for working with public housing communities.

OUT-OF-SCHOOL SUSPENSION

This manual tells "how to" form a partnership with your public/private school to serve their students on short-term suspension for no more than three weeks. Includes daily activity schedule, intake, school linkage and evaluation forms. Information contains possible source of funds as well as "how-to" introduce program to school.

TRUANCY PREVENTION

This manual gives information on "how to" operate a family-focused program for parents of children K-6 grades who miss school excessively. Includes curriculum, intake and evaluation forms, goals and objectives for a 12-week intervention leading to a graduation. A sample graduation program, volunteer support forms, resources required on "how to" get them are in there too. Truancy among youth is a national concern. You can help make a difference with this manual in hand.

JOB READINESS AND RETENTION

This manual tells "how to" operate a "soft skills" development program for individuals going from welfare to work and those who want better jobs. A 20-day curriculum with activities; intake, assessment, and evaluation forms; class calendar and attendance sheet are included. It gives information on possible sources of funds and "how-to" pursue them. With welfare reforms enacted in this country, this manual will help you help those who are most vulnerable, children, by helping their parents.

MARRIAGE GLUE

This book is full of wisdom and practical principles that can be applied to marriages regardless of age, race or cultural background. So if you feel that your marriage could use a little mending or just some added support, you may find the glue you need in these pages.

Exciting titles
by Tommy Tenney

▬ GOD'S FAVORITE HOUSE

The burning desire of your heart can be fulfilled. God is looking for people just like you. He is a Lover in search of a people who will love Him in return. He is far more interested in you than He is interested in a building. He would hush all of Heaven's hosts to listen to your voice raised in heartfelt love songs to Him. This book will show you how to build a house of worship within, fulfilling your heart's desire and His!
ISBN 0-7684-2043-1

▬ THE GOD CHASERS (Best-selling **Destiny Image** book)

There are those so hungry, so desperate for His presence, that they become consumed with finding Him. Their longing for Him moves them to do what they would otherwise never do: Chase God. But what does it really mean to chase God? Can He be "caught"? Is there an end to the thirsting of man's soul for Him? Meet Tommy Tenney—God chaser. Join him in his search for God. Follow him as he ignores the maze of religious tradition and finds himself, not chasing God, but to his utter amazement, caught by the One he had chased.
ISBN 0-7684-2016-4
Also available in Spanish
ISBN 0-7899-0642-2

▬ GOD CHASERS DAILY MEDITATION & PERSONAL JOURNAL

Does your heart yearn to have an intimate relationship with your Lord? Perhaps you long to draw closer to your heavenly Father, but you don't know how or where to start. This *Daily Meditation & Personal Journal* will help you begin a journey that will change your life. As you read and journal, you'll find your spirit running to meet Him with a desire and fervor you've never before experienced. Let your heart hunger propel you into the chase of your life...after God!
ISBN 0-7684-2040-7

▬ SECRET SOURCES OF POWER

by T.F. Tenney with Tommy Tenney.
Everyone is searching for power. People are longing for some external force to empower their lives and transform their circumstances. *Secret Sources of Power* furnishes some of the keys that will unlock the door to Divine power. You might be surprised at what is on the other side of that door. It will be the opposite of the world's concepts of power and how to obtain it. You will discover that before you lay hold of God's power you must let go of your own resources. You will be challenged to go down before you can be lifted up. Death always comes before resurrection. If you are dissatisfied with your life and long for the power of God to be manifested in you then now is the time. Take the keys and open the door to *Secret Sources of Power*!
ISBN 0-7684-5000-4

Available at your local Christian bookstore.

Destiny Image titles
you will enjoy reading

NO MORE SOUR GRAPES
by Don Nori.
Who among us wants our children to be free from the struggles we have had to bear? Who among us wants the lives of our children to be full of victory and love for their Lord? Who among us wants the hard-earned lessons from our lives given freely to our children? All these are not only possible, they are also God's will. You can be one of those who share the excitement and joy of seeing your children step into the destiny God has for them. If you answered "yes" to these questions, the pages of this book are full of hope and help for you and others just like you.
ISBN 0-7684-2037-7

THE BATTLE FOR THE SEED
by Dr. Patricia Morgan.
The dilemma facing young people today is a major concern for all parents. This important book shows God's way to change the condition of the young and advance God's purpose for every nation into the next century.
ISBN 1-56043-099-0

SOLDIERS WITH LITTLE FEET
by Dian Layton.
Every time God pours out His Spirit, the adult generation moves on without its children. Dian pleads with the Church to bring the children into the fullness of God with them and offers practical guidelines for doing so.
ISBN 0-914903-86-1

CHILDREN OF REVIVAL
by Vann Lane.
What do you do with hundreds of children during services that last for hours? At first Pastor Vann Lane thought he would use all his usual "stuff" to entertain the children. The Lord thought differently. In this book you'll read remarkable stories of Brownsville Assembly's 11-year-old leader, the worship band of young musicians, and the 75-member prayer team of children between ages 8 and 12 years old. *Children of Revival* will forever change the way you view the Church's little members.
ISBN 1-56043-699-9

Available at your local Christian bookstore.

For more information and sample chapters, visit www.destinyimage.com

6B-2:51

Destiny Image titles
you will enjoy reading

These titles are real food for the hungry heart!

SECRETS OF THE MOST HOLY PLACE
by Don Nori.
Here is a prophetic parable you will read again and again. The winds of God are blowing, drawing you to His Life within the Veil of the Most Holy Place. There you begin to see as you experience a depth of relationship your heart has yearned for. This book is a living, dynamic experience with God!
ISBN 1-56043-076-1

DIGGING THE WELLS OF REVIVAL
by Lou Engle.
Did you know that just beneath your feet are deep wells of revival? God is calling us today to unstop the wells and reclaim the spiritual inheritance of our nation, declares Lou Engle. As part of the pastoral staff at Harvest Rock Church and founder of its "24-Hour House of Prayer," he has experienced firsthand the importance of knowing and praying over our spiritual heritage. Let's renew covenant with God, reclaim our glorious roots, and believe for the greatest revival the world has ever known!
ISBN 0-7684-2015-6

WOMEN ON THE FRONT LINES
by Michal Ann Goll.
History is filled with ordinary women who have changed the course of their generation. Here Michal Ann Goll, co-founder of Ministry to the Nations with her husband, Jim, shares how her own life was transformed and highlights nine women whose lives will impact yours! Every generation faces the same choices and issues; learn how you, too, can heed the call to courage and impact a generation.
ISBN 0-7684-2020-2

WOMAN: HER PURPOSE, POSITION, AND POWER
by Mary Jean Pidgeon.
When the enemy slipped into the garden, he robbed Eve and all her daughters of their original purpose, position, and power. But today God is bringing these truths back to women. He is setting His daughters free and showing them their value in His Kingdom. Let Mary Jean Pidgeon, a wife, mother, and the Associate Pastor with her husband Pastor Jack Pidgeon in Houston, explain a woman's *purpose*, *position*, and *power*.
ISBN 1-56043-330-2

RELEASERS OF LIFE
by Mary Audrey Raycroft.
Inside you is a river that is waiting to be tapped—the river of the Holy Spirit and power! Let Mary Audrey Raycroft, a gifted exhorter and teacher and the Pastor of Equipping Ministries and Women in Ministry at the Toronto Airport Christian Fellowship, teach you how you can release the unique gifts and anointings that the Lord has placed within you. Discover how you can move and minister in God's freeing power and be a releaser of life!
ISBN 1-56043-198-9

Available at your local Christian bookstore.

For more information and sample chapters, visit www.destinyimage.com

6B-2:69

Exciting titles
by T.D. Jakes

Exciting titles
by Dr. Myles Munroe

━ UNDERSTANDING YOUR POTENTIAL

This is a motivating, provocative look at the awesome potential trapped within you, waiting to be realized. This book will cause you to be uncomfortable with your present state of accomplishment and dissatisfied with resting on your past success.

ISBN 1-56043-046-X

━ RELEASING YOUR POTENTIAL

Here is a complete, integrated, principles-centered approach to releasing the awesome potential trapped within you. If you are frustrated by your dreams, ideas, and visions, this book will show you a step-by-step pathway to releasing your potential and igniting the wheels of purpose and productivity.

ISBN 1-56043-072-9

━ MAXIMIZING YOUR POTENTIAL

Are you bored with your latest success? Maybe you're frustrated at the prospect of retirement. This book will refire your passion for living! Learn to maximize the God-given potential lying dormant inside you through the practical, integrated, and penetrating concepts shared in this book. Go for the max—die empty!

ISBN 1-56043-105-9

━ SINGLE, MARRIED, SEPARATED & LIFE AFTER DIVORCE

Written by best-selling author Myles Munroe, this is one of the most important books you will ever read. It answers hard questions with compassion, biblical truth, and even a touch of humor. It, too, is rapidly becoming a best-seller.

ISBN 1-56043-094-X

━ IN PURSUIT OF PURPOSE

Best-selling author Myles Munroe reveals here the key to personal fulfillment: purpose. We must pursue purpose because our fulfillment in life depends upon our becoming what we were born to be and do. *In Pursuit of Purpose* will guide you on that path to finding purpose.

ISBN 1-56043-103-2

━ THE PURPOSE AND POWER OF PRAISE & WORSHIP

God's greatest desire and man's greatest need is for a Spirit to spirit relationship. God created an environment of His Presence in which man is to dwell and experience the fullness of this relationship. In this book, Dr. Munroe will help you discover this experience in your daily life. You are about to discover the awesome purpose and power of praise and worship.

ISBN 0-7684-2047-4

Available at your local Christian bookstore.